The Classroom Troubleshooter

Strategies for dealing with marking and paperwork, discipline, evaluation, and learning through language

Les Parsons

Pembroke Publishers Limited

*My utmost gratitude once again to Susan Clifton for her
guidance, assistance, and support during all stages of this manuscript.*

© 2003 Pembroke Publishers
538 Hood Road
Markham, Ontario, Canada L3R 3K9
www.pembrokepublishers.com

Distributed in the U.S. by Stenhouse Publishers
477 Congress Street
Portland, ME 04101
www.stenhouse.com

Every effort has been made to contact copyright holders for permission
to reproduce borrowed material. The publishers apologize for any such
omissions and will be pleased to rectify them in subsequent reprints of
the book.

We acknowledge the financial support of the Government of Canada
through the Book Publishing Industry Development Program (BPIDP)
for our publishing activities.

We acknowledge the Government of Ontario through the Ontario
Media Development Corporation's Ontario Book Initiative.

Thanks to teacher Susan Clifton and the students of Crescent Town P.S.
who are featured on the cover.

National Library of Canada Cataloguing in Publication

Parsons, Les
    The classroom troubleshooter: strategies for marking and
paperwork, discipline, evaluation and learning through
language / Les Parsons.

For use in grades K-12.
Includes bibliographical references and index.
ISBN 1-55138-162-1

    1. Education, Elementary. 2. Education, Secondary. 3. Elementary
school teaching. 4. High school teaching. 5. Classroom management.
I. Title.

LB3013.P37 2003   372.13   C2003-902738-4

Editor: Kate Revington
Cover Design: John Zehethofer
Cover Photography: Ajay Photographics
Typesetting: Jay Tee Graphics Ltd.

Printed and bound in Canada
9 8 7 6 5 4 3 2 1

Contents

Preface

When prospective teachers daydream about teaching, they imagine themselves as "the sage on the stage," imparting knowledge and wisdom to a small cluster of eager, upturned faces. They rarely, if ever, imagine that the profession has another, darker side or that they might need a set of specialized skills to cope with it.

It may not be until they are in the classroom that teachers discover how classroom life can be a miasma of minutiae, deadlines, frustrations, roadblocks, and disturbances. *The Classroom Troubleshooter*, a road map out of that swamp and onto solid ground, is intended for those teachers.

The Classroom Troubleshooter deals with the nitty-gritty of life in the educational trenches: crowded classrooms, constant interruptions, incessant demands, inappropriate student behavior, ever-increasing "administrivia," and the number one bane of a teacher's existence: marking. It provides practical strategies that will enable teachers to restore order out of mailbox chaos, mark "smart," short-circuit discipline problems, organize classrooms to maximize learning, create an atmosphere of cooperation and trust, and devise an evaluation system that directs and stimulates learning.

Beyond that, *The Classroom Troubleshooter* empowers teachers to control their environment and to reclaim time and energy so that their skills and gifts can be directed where they are most needed: into teaching and learning alongside their students.

1

The Paper Chase

"Marking, reports, 'administrivia': the paperwork never ends!
Phone calls, meetings, photocopying:
I'm constantly running just to stay in one place!
How do I juggle all these tasks and still find time to teach?"

Most schools are prime examples of Chaos theory in action. From the moment the clamorous, irrepressible river of students floods the hallways in the morning until the last tired trickle escapes at the end of the day, whatever can happen will happen.

Whatever can happen will happen.

Consider the beginning of a typical day. You signed out the VCR for first period, but someone else took it. The photocopier jammed again and you couldn't run off the test you needed for second period. The parents of the student you kicked out of class yesterday are coming in to see you and the principal at lunchtime. Your report cards are due in the office, but you still need to mark the projects stacked on your desk before you can complete them. Finally, the vice-principal wants to see three of your students about some graffiti found in the washroom.

To give yourself time to track down the missing VCR, you assign seatwork at the start of period one. A forest of hands waves in the air, and as you acknowledge them, one by one, you hear:

"I don't know what to do."
"Can I get a drink?"
"Have you marked the test we did yesterday?"
"When's this due?"
"How do you do number 6?"
"Is this for homework if we don't finish?"
"What was the page number?"
"Can I go to the washroom?"
"Does this count for the report cards?"
"Frank just called me a pig!"
"Somebody took my book."
"My dad says you don't teach right and that's why I get low marks!"

Day-to-day teaching is an unpredictable, fly-by-the-seat-of-your-pants, emotionally draining ride through a maelstrom.

Far from being a prescribed, dispassionate, and tightly controlled presentation of ordered elements, day-to-day teaching is an unpredictable, fly-by-the-seat-of-your-pants, emotionally draining ride through a maelstrom. A lot of what teachers do in the name of instruction, however, has surprisingly little to do with teaching. Most people equate teaching with designing and presenting lessons. Too often, teachers are "winging it," delivering lessons off the top of their heads. They have little choice. Somehow, they have to accommodate a host of tasks and responsibilities competing for the same, limited out-of-class time. These obligations and undertakings, which encompass administration, supervision, extracurricular activities and communication/collaboration, range in importance from essential to peripheral, but all of them require a teacher's attention.

Do these administrative tasks sound familiar?

- Keep daily attendance records.
- Mark work.
- Record marks and transcribe observations.
- Read and attend to daily mail (staff and board memos, a variety of board newsletters, phone messages from parents/guardians, instructions for special excursions and events, and questionnaires).
- Prepare trip permission forms (type, print, copy); distribute and collect forms; assess allergies, special needs, and risks; arrange for parent volunteers; prepare a bus seating plan as required; arrange placement and work for students not going.
- Order supplies and instructional materials.
- Gather resources and equipment.
- Prepare and photocopy instructional materials and tests.
- Maintain and repair computers.

Consider these supervision duties:

- Oversee yard, hall, lunchroom, buses, dances, and concerts before, during and after school.
- Cover "on calls" (supplying for a colleague when no occasional teacher is available).
- Monitor study and detention rooms.
- Address inappropriate behavior in all classes and in halls throughout the day on an ad hoc basis, including during prep periods, recess breaks, and lunch periods.

Remember extracurricular activities, which are often conducted over an extended period, before or after the instructional day, or possibly during lunch hours.

- Supervise, maintain, and distribute equipment, uniforms, musical instruments, supplies, and other resources.
- Coach students at practices and games, and also deal with transportation and communication with parents and guardians about their children's involvement.
- Play a role in organizing, instructing, and supervising clubs, dances, concerts, and overnight excursions.

Finally, don't forget about communication/collaboration, which typically occurs before or after the instructional day or possibly during lunch hours.

- Telephone, write, and meet with parents or guardians on an ad hoc basis.
- Write report cards.
- Meet with guidance counsellors, administrators and other support personnel.
- Attend staff meetings, as well as grade and subject meetings, with other teachers.
- Attend in-services and workshops (often held after school or on Saturdays).
- Serve on school committees, such as staffing, budget, equity, and special events.
- Act as subject-specific staff liaison with board departments; receive and disseminate information in such areas as reading, math, science, visual arts, and social sciences.
- Arrange for field trips and excursions.

If you're a teacher and you need to create order out of this chaos, where do you start?

When teachers gripe about lacking time to teach, they're voicing their frustration with this barrage of out-of-class duties that compete with time needed for the detailed planning, preparation, and formative assessment that lie at the heart of the teaching process. Generating long-term plans, creating detailed lesson plans, and maintaining a comprehensive daybook too often fall into a category called wishful thinking.

If you're a teacher and you need to create order out of this chaos, where do you start?

The best place to begin is your office mailbox. Before you mark your first quiz, see your first student, and even plan your first lesson, you have to empty your office mailbox. Like a magician's top hat, your mailbox has mysteriously filled over the summer months, and no matter how often you empty it, you'll find it filled next time you look. A mail cubicle is a Pandora's box of phone messages, office memoranda, reminders, schedules, timetables, questionnaires, forms, student records, and catalogues. The struggle for order begins every year and each day at your mailbox.

Whatever its source and quantity, though, paper is merely marshalled in a teacher's mailbox, resting temporarily before moving on to its ultimate destination, the teacher's desk. Most teachers realize that creating a paper avalanche on top of their desks invites disaster; the few who claim to be able to put their hands on any item they need from the stack are lying. Everybody needs a filing system.

A Place for Everything

The system that most teachers come up with seems self-evident. Everybody has filing cabinets; everybody has "stuff" they need to file. The obvious solution is to dump the "stuff," albeit alphabetically, in the filing cabinets.

There are a few problems with alphabetical filing, though. One problem is that it's too tempting in the name of "efficiency" to let the paper accumulate on top of your desk and file only periodically, perhaps once a term. Another problem is that Test scores, for example, are inevitably lumped in with Thanksgiving lessons, Telephone numbers, Timetables, Tracking sheets, and more. Teachers laboriously shift through the clutter in their filing cabinets every time they need something, often uncovering an item they needed last week, but couldn't find.

The trick with filing is organizing space for materials in a manner that suits your needs. For teachers, that means a system that is carefully and specifically categorized, instantly and easily accessible, and completely flexible. Filing in three-ring binders achieves all of these goals. The binders can be categorized according to need, such as daybook, staff meetings, office memos, professional development, marks and anecdotal records, parental contacts, lesson plans, resources, or evaluation masters. Almost anything, such as photocopies, schedules, computer hard copies, or even catalogues, can be punched and instantly filed. Hard-to-file items, such as phone messages or receipts, can be taped onto blank 8½ by 11 inch pages. Items can be added anywhere in the binder and pages can be removed promptly. The system is flexible.

The binders most in use can be arrayed standing up, spine labels showing, across the back of your desk; others can be stored in a desk drawer or filing cabinet. Either way, the contents are instantly accessible. Three-ring binders provide a place for everything and ensure that everything is in its proper place.

The next step is to efficiently activate and maintain this system.

Four Options for Paper

When paper comes into your hands, you have four options: (1) dispose of it immediately; (2) file it, either in full view or in your filing system; (3) act on it immediately; or (4) act on it later. As long as you're decisive, clinical, and consistent, you will quickly control the paper flow.

When paper comes into your hands, you have four options.

Of the four options, the first is the simplest and most effective. Read the paper. If it requires no action and if you don't need it later, throw it away. Immediately. Weed your files before the paper ever reaches them. The only problem is that you can never tell what you may need in the future. If you listen to that nibbling inner voice, however, your files will soon become unmanageable. Based on what you know now, if you can't see yourself needing or acting on the information, throw it away. If the information turns out to be important at some future date, be assured that someone will send it to you again or you can access it some other way. Vital information is easily obtained.

The second option is equally straightforward. If the paper requires no action, but you will need it for future reference, file it in the appropriate binder or post it in plain view on a wall or bulletin board around your desk. Posting items that need to be referenced daily or weekly avoids constantly accessing your binders for the same purpose. Duty schedules, frequently used telephone numbers, timetables, or fire routines are some of the kinds of paper that should be available at a glance. If you leave them lying on your desk, you can be sure that something else will cover them up and they'll be gone the next time you need them. Be selective, as well, or you won't see the trees for the forest.

The third option, the one teachers dread, is most responsible for a paper log-jam. If the paper requires action, act on it, if at all possible, immediately. When teachers are multi-tasking, they can always find a good excuse for not dealing with paper: the good excuse, however, is not always a valid reason. Efficient teachers adhere to the old adage of touching paper once. If it's a questionnaire, book order, note from a peer, checklist, office request, or any of a host of other items requiring your attention, aim to respond to it immediately. If it's a reminder of something you need to do on a subsequent day, put it in your day-book for that particular day. Don't let these pile up on your desk. If you can't attend to the task that minute, keep a To Do Today tray and resolve never to go home without emptying it. That resolution alone will prod you to act on items without delay.

Finally, you may receive paper that requires your attention, but not immediately. A good rule of thumb is, if you can, act on it immediately anyway. If you can't, keep another tray on your desk marked To Do This Week and drop it there. Remind yourself each morning and evening that you won't go home on Friday until that tray is empty. If you stick to that resolution and continue to exercise your four options deliberately and conscientiously, your paper will vanish.

Logging Parental Contacts

What parents do know is that they want to speak directly to their child's teacher about an issue they think is important.

An essential corollary to the immediate action rule involves returning telephone messages from parents and guardians. Parents don't usually call the school. When they do, they might be calling about a poor test result, a request for homework, some difficulty at home, a conflict with another student or another teacher, or a garbled or confusing tale the student has taken home. When they do call, they usually want to speak to the teacher as soon as possible.

Unfortunately, parents usually don't understand how schools operate. They don't realize that a teacher may not have a chance to retrieve the phone message taken by a school secretary at 9 a.m. until some time that afternoon. They may not be aware that on any particular day a teacher may be unable to phone until the end of the school day. They are also not considering the other phone messages, the hall, yard, and lunchroom duties, the formal and informal meetings, and the thousand and one chores and tasks that fill up the times when a teacher isn't with a class.

What parents *do* know is that they want to speak directly to their child's teacher about an issue they think is important. Parents also understand what it means to be slighted or ignored. Whatever issue is on a parent's mind at 9 a.m. will fester all day until it's resolved. The more they feel they're being neglected, the more their mood will darken.

Teachers need to get into the habit of checking their mailboxes frequently. Checking first thing in the morning, around mid-day, and after school will keep you on top of the constant flow of paper and, in the case of phone messages, will short-circuit any parent's rising impatience and worry.

Return calls from parents promptly, at least the same day or the same morning or afternoon the message is relayed. Sooner is even better. Procrastination has serious implications. If you expect a problem arising from the phone call, delaying will only exacerbate the problem by increasing the parent's agitation. If it's not a problem, delaying may turn it into one. The longer that parents have to wait for a return call, the less value they assume the teacher places on their requests or concerns. Your association and relationship with parents is vitally important in your efforts to educate their children. If parents have something to say important enough for them to call you, demonstrate by your actions that it's important to you to hear them.

Whether a parent or guardian telephones you or you call the home, you must keep a written record of the call, the content, and what transpired. Be sure to keep those notes in the same place that you keep all your records of parental contacts, as well as your anecdotal comments about your students.

Consistent with your binder filing system, prepare a binder beforehand with several pages set aside for each student. As well as including written records of parental contacts, you can log relevant observations, noteworthy reminders, such as extracurricular interests or achievements, concerns brought forward from other teachers, peer conflicts, or out-of-the-ordinary occurrences. You could also include labelled photocopies of significant or characteristic work.

These records are invaluable during any kind of reporting or decision-making conferences, such as parent-teacher conferences, student-teacher conferences, grade, placement, or promotional meetings, or inquiries from guidance counsellors or administration. Everyone involved in the student's education can use these critical observations to flesh out the two-dimensional picture offered by a series of marks and grades.

A student's isolated behavior on any given day can also be placed into a context over time as part of the anecdotal records. Have your misgivings about a student's behavior been echoed by others? Is the behavior isolated or part of a pattern? Have the parents been informed? What concerns, if any, have the parents expressed? These kinds of questions are automatically answered if your anecdotal records are kept up-to-date and complete.

Pages 13 to 14 show sample anecdotal records of a student's behavior and the related record of parental contact. Blank photocopiable forms appear as appendices.

Climbing the Marking Mountain

Even if you get that huge rock of marking rolled to the top of the hill at the end of the day, it's waiting for you next morning right back at the bottom.

No matter how accomplished you become at organizing the paper flow and systematizing information input, unless you can deal with the daunting reality of marking, all your juggling will be in vain. Keep in mind that evaluation and marking are two ends of the same horse. Evaluation is the head, leading and directing the horse's learning processes. Marking is what spills out of the other end after the learning is digested. The classroom teacher is the faithful attendant following behind with a shovel and pail. Although Chapter 3 details the essential ingredients in creating a comprehensive, effective evaluation system, marking is simply a matter of pushing more paper.

Make no mistake: Marking is a Sisyphian task. Even if you get that huge rock of marking rolled to the top of the hill at the end of the day, it's waiting for you next morning right back at the bottom. Marking is time-consuming, never-ending, and often mind-numbingly boring.

If you happen to discover a routine that allows you to keep up with the daily grind of marking notebooks, homework assignments, daily assignments, and quizzes, you then call in a major project or give an exam. Somehow, you have to continue the daily marking, which you are just managing to do while attending to this even more important marking chore. The grades, of course, are vital for the completion of report cards that are due in the office on Friday. Since you won't have time to do your daily marking when you're preparing report cards, the pile of notebooks and papers in your In tray begins to threaten the ceiling.

Anecdotal Records

Student name: *Troy Harrington*

A. Notation: *- Eng. homework incomplete; second time this week*

    Date: *September 12th*

B. Notation: *- plagiarized composition; sample enclosed, parents informed*

    Date: *September 18th*

C. Notation: *- constantly late for Science class; teacher complained, Guidance notified*

    Date: *September 23rd*

D. Notation: *- copied someone else's History homework; teacher complained, Guidance and parents informed*

    Date: *September 25th*

E. Notation: *- meeting with Guidance/parents; testing agreed on for possible learning disability; remedial routine established*

    Date: *September 30th*

Contact with Parent/Guardian

Student name: *Troy Harrington*

Adult contact: *Mrs. J. Harrington (parent)*

Date: *September 25*

Type of contact: Check the appropriate box.

telephone to ❑   phone from ❑   interview ❑

written note to ❑   written note from ❑

agenda note to ❑   agenda note from ❑

Issue:

1. History teacher reports that Troy copied another student's homework.

2. Pattern of Troy's difficulties and frustrations with school work emerging.

Relevant details:

Parents are concerned about Troy's adjustment to his new school. He has had difficulties in the past, but these have been resolved when parents and school develop routines for daily communication.

Proposed action (if any):

Meeting with parents and guidance counsellor scheduled for September 30 in Guidance office at 4:30 p.m. to discuss emerging concerns and possible interventions.

Date action taken (if applicable):   d _30_   m _09_   y 20 _03_

On the one hand, the ongoing, career-long task of marking is formidable and daunting; on the other hand, the necessity to remain up-to-date with it is inescapable. The perpetual burden drives some teachers to devise ingenious, if self-defeating, ways to relieve the stress.

The magically expanding marking bag: The teacher puts each day's marking in a bag or briefcase and carries it from the classroom to the lunchroom, from the lunchroom to the staff room, from the staff room to the classroom, and finally drags it home. Each morning four or five pieces of marked work are returned to students and thirty new pieces are added. While the marking bag grows heavier, the teacher maintains the illusion that the problem is being resolved.

The "open door" marking system: Wherever the teacher chooses to mark, innumerable interruptions lie in wait. A classroom with an open door, a shared office, the staff room or lunchroom, and the family room at home offer distractions that defeat the teacher's best intentions. Depending on the setting, informal meetings with colleagues, televisions shows, school gossip, and household crises can conspire to stretch a five-minute marking task into a two-hour period of spinning one's wheels. Little is accomplished, but at least it isn't the teacher's fault.

The "I'll get to it later" syndrome: This avoidance technique carries with it an air of professional indignation that effectively masks the obvious procrastination. The teacher wants to get at that marking, but has a number of more important duties that demand attention: planning, daybook, baseball practice, phone calls, e-mail checking, file organizing, e-mail checking again, filing cabinet dusting, a new bulletin board display, or help with someone else's volleyball practice. This teacher never expects or understands the criticism levelled by students, parents, and administration as the unmarked work gathers dust.

The pressures of marking have also moulded classroom management and instructional practices. Marking, for instance, drives the time-honored concept of seatwork. As the name implies, seatwork is any activity, usually written, that students are expected to complete at their desks with little supervision. While the students are thus occupied, the teacher marks the previous lesson. After a period of time, the teacher collects the seatwork, teaches a new concept, assigns new seatwork based on that concept, and marks the work just collected. In the case of split grades, the teacher assigns "seatwork" to one grade and teaches a lesson to the other grade. While the second grade is completing their seatwork, the first grade receives another lesson, and so on. While meaningful applications and activities can certainly occur within this organization, always keep in mind that the technique arose out of a necessity, not choice.

It's true that teachers need to manage their classrooms efficiently. Marking has to be handled like any other assembly-line operation. Unlike in a cookie factory, where the workers adjust to the demands of the assembly line, though, teachers have a choice: you can be at the mercy of the assembly line or you can choose to control the line. Before your first class each year, you know two things about marking: it's coming and it won't stop coming until the year is over. With that in mind, you can plan how to control input to manage output. Whether you teach the same subject to four or more classes or all subjects to one class, you can manipulate the type of marking you do and the speed with which you do it.

When to Let Students Mark

Too often, daily marking assumes a ritualistic pattern: students have the responsibility for churning out a product and teachers accept the responsibility for marking it. In many cases, however, you can take the responsibility for marking off your shoulders. You can let students mark their own work, so that they can know right away how well they're doing and whether or not they're on the right track.

Whether or not you want students to mark their own work depends on your intent behind the marking.

Whether or not you want students to mark their own work depends on your intent behind the marking. With the marking of daily work, your intent is usually formative: you're trying to help students determine what they know and know how to do and what they may need to review. In these cases, since it's neither necessary nor productive to keep records of how well students are progressing, let them mark their own work. You can read aloud the correct answers or responses, put them on an overhead projector, or hand out photocopied answer sheets. Homework assignments, trial dictations, or brief, informal quizzes are some of the situations that lend themselves to students marking their own work. The students get instant feedback and the responsibility for marking is placed on their shoulders. Even if they correct mistakes as they mark or revise their final score, they have still attended to what they did or didn't know. The goal of the marking is realized. (Chapter 3 provides a more detailed explanation of the differences between formative and summative evaluation.)

As a teacher, you have a variety of reasons for often marking work yourself. Sometimes, the marking may require a teacher's knowledge, experience, sophisticated decision-making skills, or concentrated focus. Sometimes, you need to take an individual student's needs and abilities into account as you mark. At other times, you may want to check on students' thinking processes as they work through problems, assess their progress, or monitor your program's effectiveness.

Some teachers, on the other hand, indulge in the practice of students marking other students' work. They either have students trade papers or enlist "star" students to act as surrogate teacher markers. When students mark other students' work, however, the message is clear: you want to use the marks for summative evaluation purposes and you think they'll cheat if they mark their own. Some students certainly might, if given the opportunity. Placing everyone under that shadow of doubt, however, undermines and devalues the quality of trust and cooperation you are trying to engender in your classroom.

You also break the bond of confidentiality and open students to the possibilities of humiliation and coercion. A student's personal and private academic struggles could easily become public on the whim of a peer. Imagine, as well, the pressures, including friendship, under which students mark the work of peers they like, dislike, fear, or admire.

Meanwhile, since few students have the motivation, maturity, or skill required to apply themselves assiduously to marking, students often make mistakes when marking other students' work. To offset this tendency, some teachers fall into the trap of enforcing a system of negative penalties. Students making mistakes marking other students' work lose marks from their own papers. When a student receives a lower grading as a result of a mistake in marking made on someone else's paper, evaluation loses any semblance of relevance, objectivity, or fairness. Regardless of whether or not the marking is for formative or summative purposes or whether one student or all students are involved, the practice of students marking other students' work should be avoided.

Meeting Your Daily Marking Quota

If you can't get students to do the marking for you, how do you keep up with the avalanche of routine marking that envelops you every day? Notebooks are the worst, from subject-specific notebooks, such as History or English, to journals of all kinds, including work diaries and lab reports. Miss them for one day and you're snowed under; the longer you leave them, the longer it takes you to catch up.

The key to keeping up is finding a workable routine and sticking to it.

Collecting a set of notebooks every three or four weeks has several drawbacks. With up to a dozen entries for each one, the time and effort required to mark one class set — let alone three or four — is preclusive. Besides, with that length of time between markings, students have little chance of benefiting from formative evaluation and improving their performance.

The key to keeping up is finding a workable routine and sticking to it. Most teachers find that if they mark five or six notebooks from each class every second day or a couple of notebooks each day, they're able to stay current. In some cases, a simple comment or question on a Post-it note may be all that's required.

Marking the content in daily notebooks is more problematic. Teachers want to let students know how well they're functioning and what they need to do to improve. They also need to keep the marking fast and efficient to stay on top of the quantity of material.

Devising a simple rubric containing performance criteria and achievement levels is a popular solution. A check mark or color code indicates to students how well they're progressing. Students glue or staple the rubric into the notebook and complete items, such as date, unit to be marked (or pages to be marked if notebooks are paginated), and self-evaluation sections, before submitting the notebook for marking.

A comment section allows the teacher to personalize or extend the evaluation. A self-evaluation component affords students an opportunity to assess for themselves the extent to which they've achieved their learning objectives and to assume some responsibility for the worth of the work.

The easy-to-mark rubric on page 18 contains all the information necessary for students to understand what they need to do to improve. It also helps guide the teacher's summative notebook evaluation at a later date.

Rubric for Notebook Marking

Date: _____

Unit marked: _____ Topic: _____ from page _____ to page _____

Content: Self-evaluation	All	Most	Some	None
* basic assignments completed	❏	❏	❏	❏
* responses detailed, thorough	❏	❏	❏	❏
* responses thoughtful, insightful	❏	❏	❏	❏
* optional assignments completed	❏	❏	❏	❏
* optional responses detailed, thorough	❏	❏	❏	❏
* optional responses thoughtful, insightful	❏	❏	❏	❏

Editing/Proofreading: Self-evaluation	Very Effective	Effective	Ineffective
* spelling, punctuation, other usage — level of conventional use	❏	❏	❏

Content: Teacher Evaluation	All	Most	Some	None
* basic assignments completed	❏	❏	❏	❏
* responses detailed, thorough	❏	❏	❏	❏
* responses thoughtful, insightful	❏	❏	❏	❏
* optional assignments completed	❏	❏	❏	❏
* optional responses detailed, thorough	❏	❏	❏	❏
* optional responses thoughtful, insightful				

Editing/Proofreading: Teacher Evaluation	Very Effective	Effective	Ineffective
* spelling, punctuation, other usage — level of conventional use	❏	❏	❏

Teacher Comment: _____

_____

_____

Marking "Smart"

Another problematic aspect of marking is the kind of marking teachers do. Too many teachers spend too much of their valuable time editing the surface features of their students' written work. Marking pens in hand, day after day, they meticulously hunt through class set after class set of notebooks and essays, tracking down every spelling mistake, punctuation error, or usage and grammar lapse. This kind of marking is one of the least efficient and effective possible uses of a teacher's time and talents.

Except in the case of work made public, such as the publishing of compositions, daily work doesn't need to be "camera-ready." Unless something about the correction process intrinsically benefits students, a perfect draft is unnecessary. When English teachers, for example, insist on a final, well-edited draft, they guide students through a student-centred writing process based on self- and peer-editing. The degree to which students are able to effectively edit their own work is a component of the mark given the final draft. Students write, revise, and edit; English teachers evaluate the process and the product.

Too many teachers in subject areas other than English must believe that a close marking of surface errors is an essential learning/teaching strategy. Although unsupported by any research or evidence, these teachers are convinced that unless students correct these kinds of mistakes, they will keep making them. In an effort to compel conventional usage and prevent the recurrence of errors, they direct students through a repetitive, mindless process of correction.

If teachers truly believed in this practice, they wouldn't get so frustrated as students *do* make the same mistakes over and again or create new errors while correcting the errors pointed out to them. This practice does not develop in students the motivation, confidence, skills, and practice required to shape and monitor their own writing; rather, it discourages risk taking, encourages a warped view of the writing process, and stunts growth in writing skills.

Marking "smart" . . . means focusing on the content and providing students with much needed feedback on the strengths and weaknesses of their work.

With all that marking of surface errors, though, teachers are certainly honing their own editing/proofreading skills; they are also providing concrete proof to parents and supervisors alike that they are actively on the job. Marking "smart," on the other hand, means focusing on the content and providing students with much needed feedback on the strengths and weaknesses of their work. It means refusing to become an unpaid, unquestioning, bleary-eyed editor and proofreader.

Marking Tests and Exams

Here's a classic marking conundrum. You've just spent a week marking a series of tests or mid-term exams; of course, during that week your classes have continued to churn out daily work in their notebooks, journals, or lab manuals. You now have a week's backlog of daily marking. Unless you plan to give yourself some breathing space, you'll never get off the marking treadmill and you'll never get caught up. If you resort to a week of games, such as word searches and crosswords, you lose valuable learning/teaching time, devalue the nature of learning in your classroom, and probably promote discipline problems when your students realize they're putting in time with meaningless busywork. For a simple solution, go to your curriculum.

When you schedule an evaluation period, plan some program modifications right after the testing. Introduce a unit that doesn't require daily marking, such as a series of hands-on experiments, manipulations, or construction activities. An oral report, a research project with a comprehensive, but easily marked evaluation rubric, or, depending on the subject area, a design or graphic assignment would be other options. (The section called "Assigning and Marking Projects," pages 61 to 65, features an example of just such a project assignment sheet and accompanying rubric.)

Whatever the activity, your purpose is twofold: to engage your students in a legitimate and meaningful learning experience while, at the same time, reducing your daily marking quota to afford you time to complete your test or exam marking.

The sooner students get their papers back, the more they learn from the testing.

When teachers are responsible for teaching several subjects to one class, they automatically space out their tests and exams for several valid reasons. The sooner students get their papers back, the more they learn from the testing; when teachers have multiple sets of tests or exams to mark, the lag time before some sets are returned is far too long. The potential for learning through a test is seriously diminished when students are engrossed in a totally different unit or topic. Besides, the review process that students undertake before a test or exam is far more effective if they can focus on one subject area at a time.

When teachers are responsible for teaching a single subject to several classes, they would like to stagger their tests or exams, but encounter a serious problem if they do. Like it or not, at some point in their school careers, students learn that success in school means getting good grades. The older they get, the more they're pressured by teachers and parents to do better. Students who are failing are pressured to pass, students who are barely passing are pressured to get at least an average grade, and even honor students receive a "grilling" about their "lowest" subject. The only place students don't feel pressure about grades is within their peer group; from the perspective of the peer group, everyone is in the same boat and it's everyone against the system. Sharing answers or information about a test, then, becomes an expected strategy against the common foe rather than an example of cheating. Teachers quickly learn that students will exchange answers on a test even as one class exits the classroom and the next one enters. If the test is given on separate days, the problem gets worse.

The way to bring all this silliness to a halt is to tell your classes ahead of time that each class will receive a different version of the test. In the computer age, producing different versions of a test of a specific body of content is fast and efficient. Since each class receives a different test, you can stagger the testing dates, give yourself time to mark, and get the marked tests back to your classes as quickly as possible after they've handed them in. With a test of factual content, you might create four types of tests for four classes, for example, short answer, true/false, statement matching, or fill-in-the-blanks. Each class receives a different test. For the next test of new content, match each class to a type of test they haven't already received; that way, each class at some time encounters the advantages and the disadvantages of a particular test type.

With essay-type answers or compositions, consider using a marking rubric containing a self-evaluation component that students complete before handing in their papers. Page 21 shows a sample rubric. The criteria in the rubric provide a specific focus for students to assess their efforts more objectively. You'll find that, with some practice in self-evaluation, students usually assign themselves a

Marking Rubric for Expository Writing

Checking Specific Characteristics (Please circle the appropriate letter.)

V = Very Effective   **E** = Effective   **N** = Needs Improvement

	Self	Teacher	
Opening Section introduces theme of essay; gets you "hooked"; leads you on	V E N	V E N	
Argument each point leads on to the next; points make sense; persuasive; insightful	V E N	V E N	
Coherence smooth flow; sentences linked; nothing left out or out of place	V E N	V E N	
Factual Content (if applicable) correct, relevant, sufficient quantity; demonstrates comprehensive knowledge base	V E N	V E N	
Closing Section wraps it up; brings all points together; brings argument to a close	V E N	V E N	
Language vivid, colorful, apt; varied use of words, phrases, and images	V E N	V E N	
Editing/Proofreading spelling, punctuation, other usage — conventions correctly applied	V E N	V E N	

Teacher Comment:

Mark

reasonable mark based on the worth of the piece. When a significant gap is apparent between a student's self-evaluation and the teacher's evaluation, that difference can form the basis of a useful student-teacher conference. The self-evaluation component also serves as a learning/teaching tool, acquainting students with their strengths and weaknesses and directing their future studies. The final bonus with this technique is that it's easy to mark.

The best way to use this kind of marking rubric is to first give the work a grade based on a general impression after a single reading, go back and fill in the specific characteristics, and revise the mark, if necessary, after reflecting on the rubric criteria.

Marking Projects

To avoid being swamped by a class set of projects landing on your desk on the same day, let alone three or four sets, establish a series of due dates for the projects to be completed. No rule states that all students have to hand in projects on the same day. The only reason for insisting on a single due date is fairness; you don't want some students to have more time to complete the project than other students (even though you soon learn that many students will wait until the penultimate moment to begin the assignment).

Explain to your class or classes that you'll be setting a series of due dates for the projects to allow everyone to get their marked project returned soon after it's handed in. Emphasize that the first due date gives the first group or class plenty of time to complete the project and that for the next project or assignment, the group that went first this time gets the later due date.

Create a marking rubric with criteria based on the requirements and expectations of the project. Let the students see the marking rubric as soon as you offer them the explanations and instructions indicating what needs to be done and in what manner. If they know precisely the criteria by which they will be evaluated, they will more readily direct their efforts to meeting those criteria and will understand them thoroughly when self-evaluating themselves. A comprehensive example of how a rubric can be constructed to help guide and evaluate all stages of a project is found in Chapter 3, beginning on page 62.

Always encourage students to hand in work early. Tell them that first in is first marked and returned, and be sure to follow that policy. If the last one in is the first one marked, students have no motivation to hand in work before the due date. Date and number the projects (or anything else that's handed in early), and mark them in that order. At the very least, when all the projects have been handed in, you can immediately hand back the early pieces you've already marked. Most students want to know how well they did as soon as possible. When word gets around that there's a way to get material returned early, a significant number will avail themselves of the opportunity.

Beyond Crisis Management

In any endeavor, function should precede form. In teaching, the opposite often applies. You have to learn how to manage the never-ending pile of marking before you have the time or inclination to reflect on the nature of your evaluation

Always encourage students to hand in work early. Tell them that first in is first marked and returned, and be sure to follow that policy.

systems; you have to organize and systematize your record keeping before you can focus on the content of the records you're keeping. In fact, the constant barrage of secretarial, custodial, administrative, and supervisory tasks can leave you in a perpetual state of crisis management that precludes reflection. When you're treading water to keep from drowning, you're not likely to debate the educational benefits of kayaking over water polo.

In one area of teaching, however, form and function are interdependent and inseparable. The issue of discipline leads you directly into your personal educational philosophy; how you approach the issue is dependent on what you perceive your role as a teacher to be. Although discipline can be as simple and unvarying as enforcing a rigid set of rules, it can also be as complex and wide-ranging as curriculum itself. One popular definition states that curriculum is everything that happens in a school; in that sense, curriculum and discipline are two sides of the same coin. Once you've learned how to manage the daily crises that make up your typical teaching day, you know you can be a teacher. As the next chapter demonstrates, your approach to discipline will determine what kind of teacher you're going to be.

Your approach to discipline will determine what kind of teacher you're going to be.

2

The Discipline Maze

"How strict should you be with students?"
"Isn't discipline the office's problem?"
"Why should we be meddling in their private lives?"
"What can you do about the way students behave?"

In education, discipline means establishing correct order and behavior in a class-room using such methods as rules, direct instruction, and punishment. That's the only part of discipline that's relatively straightforward. Deciding how to maintain discipline is complicated; deciding when disciplinary measures are warranted can be even more perplexing.

Imagine, for example, that you teach in a junior high school. The morning bell rings. As your homeroom students enter the classroom, some of them sit down and chat quietly or pull out some work. Others don't.

- Alicia looks like she's been crying.
- Wayne and Jorge are arguing; Jorge calls Wayne "a fag."
- Robert trips Harmandeep who falls into Ian who roughly pushes Harmandeep back and Harmandeep trips over a chair.
- Jason whispers something to Sophie and Tanya; he laughs, but they blush and frown.
- Helen, Aziza, and Sasha are arguing heatedly in the hall with Keja and Mary from another class; they seem to be arguing about a rumor and you hear the word "bitch."
- Hassan, Jerry, Ashante, Carol, and Bill immediately sit down and start copy-ing last night's history homework from Natalie's notebook.
- Wan-Li and Frank saunter in and loudly slam their binders and books on their desks.

In some schools, that's a normal morning; in others, an accumulation of behaviors you might see over the course of a week. You'll also witness many other instances of questionable language, dress, and deportment, overt and subtle acts of defiance, racism, sexism, and homophobia, as well as bullying and other types of relational harassment and intimidation. When you add up the daily indica-tions of the physical, emotional, and psychological stresses and trauma to which

Deciding how to maintain discipline is complicated; deciding when disciplinary measures are warranted can be even more perplexing.

4

young people are exposed, you begin to wonder what should or could be done about it. Sooner or later, all teachers ask some disturbing questions:

- Why do young people in schools act the way they do?
- How much of their behavior in classrooms is the business of teachers?
- How much of their behavior in the hallways, lunchrooms, and schoolyards is the business of teachers?
- When should a teacher intervene in a student's private and personal life?
- When teachers decide to intervene in student behavior, how should they go about it?

You can't know how to change or even punish the behavior until you figure out the reasons behind it.

Too many people try to understand student behavior in schools in terms of opposites: good and bad, right and wrong, or reward and punishment. In this simple, linear system, teachers set and enforce the rules and students obey them. Discipline is a matter of tracing cause and effect: when students transgress, they suffer the consequences. The reality, however, is far more complex and far more difficult to understand or to supervise.

When we enclose large numbers of young people in one building day after day for years, we create a subculture that takes on a life of its own. Schools are beehives of peculiar customs, cliques, and codes built on a foundation of friendship and status and revolving around the values of the "in crowd." Interpreting, managing, and influencing behavior in this world is never straightforward.

Discipline is a problem-solving exercise. In most cases, you know what the student did. The problem is figuring out why. You can't know how to change or even punish the behavior until you figure out the reasons behind it. That's why zero tolerance policies, based on a one-size-fits-all code of conduct, are fraught with inequities. Maze-like, the search for a comprehensive approach to discipline leads in many directions at once and contains dead ends and surprises along the way.

Setting Standards

Maintaining discipline in the classroom is usually equated with being strict. Experienced teachers advise beginners to be ultra-strict in September and slowly loosen up as the year progresses. Most parents hope that their children have a strict teacher as long as the teacher is also fair. Beginning teachers wonder, "Am I strict enough or too strict?"

A more pertinent and primary question, however, might be "What do I believe is really important about the way people should interact in my classroom?" The answer to that question determines how a teacher perceives the learning/teaching environment and shapes a teacher's teaching style and approach to discipline.

At this point, a note of caution is necessary.

Before contemplating any dramatic change in the way you conduct your classroom, carefully take the measure of your students and the prevailing culture of your school. As with so many aspects of change in the educational environment, teachers need to start small, think big, and grow with their own convictions.

Students are never blank slates. Even with very young students, teachers inherit the values and behaviors set and tolerated in the home. As students move through the grades, teachers also inherit the values and behaviors set and tolerated in all the other previous classrooms as well as the culture of the school itself and the larger world beyond. Music, television, video games, movies, the Internet, and magazines are just a few of the available outlets that both shape and express young people's particular interests and mores. As a teacher, you must temper your expectations with this pre-existing conditioning.

Blanket policies set by a school or school board also affect how students and learning are perceived. Decisions made about any number of issues, from school uniforms to the format of report cards to policies on violence, can directly and indirectly influence how teachers behave toward their students, how students see their own status, and how all people in the environment interact and learn.

Keep in mind, as well, that students are wise in the ways of schools. For the most part and in most schools, they quickly learn that the kinds of negative language and behaviors that infuse the hallways, schoolyard, and cafeteria need to be moderated inside the adult-controlled, formal atmosphere of the classroom. When racist, sexist, or homophobic values and attitudes remain out of sight for extended periods, teachers can be lulled into a sense of complacency. Out of sight, however, should never be out of mind.

When silence equals consent, doing nothing is never an option.

Eventually, incidents will flare up in the classroom and the teacher had better be ready to deal with them. When silence equals consent, doing nothing is never an option. The basic principles of equity need to be supported and constantly reinforced by the classroom teacher. Empower all students by taking the following steps:

- Stop all forms of harassment, including name-calling. Every incident should be addressed and dealt with — the school environment must be made safe for all students. Those doing the harassing will receive the message that their behavior is wrong and that they must stop; those being harassed will receive the message that they have done nothing wrong and will be supported.
- Prepare your school "backups" before you need them. Talk to administrators and guidance personnel about their probable responses to the kinds of harassment you know will eventually arise. Acquaint yourself with the details of the school behavior code. Talk to other teachers about the kind of support you can expect from the school administration.
- Refuse to allow students to trivialize the behavior. Students using inappropriate language and students who are the brunt of the language will often claim that it's only a joke, no offence was meant or taken, or everybody talks like that. A fight will be characterized as "just fooling around." Someone who shouts "That's so gay!" will innocently claim that it just means "to be happy."
- Respect the confidentiality of students who describe how they have been harassed or who request help or support for friends. More severe harassment awaits anyone who blows the whistle on someone in the peer group.

Discipline is a function of program. The goals of any program should be to raise self-esteem; involve the students in worthwhile, relevant, interesting, and challenging activities; foster trust and cooperation; and eliminate stereotypes. The more the program nears those goals, the less time teachers have to spend on disciplinary issues. In too many cases, however, teachers discover roadblocks in a rigid, narrowly prescribed curriculum, a lack of resources and material support for program modifications, or an uneven, inconsistent approach to student conduct by colleagues and administrators. All these issues and more affect how much control teachers have over the programs they're expected to deliver and the manner in which their students interact.

Classrooms 'r' Us

Regardless of the status quo in a school, teachers need to be true to themselves and their professional vision. The approach to everyday learning remains critically important. When teachers organize their classrooms, they make statements about their students as learners. In contemporary classrooms, teachers lead by example. The values upon which a productive environment are based must be modelled by the teacher and consistently applied. Cooperation for the good of all and respect for self and others are essential conditions. All participants, as a matter of course, also have the right to learn together in an environment free of sexist, racial, social, and cultural stereotypes. These characteristics form the true classroom basics.

Keep in mind, as well, that you are constantly sending subliminal messages to your students. While you're busy learning everything that you can about thirty to one hundred or more students, they are focused intently on you: what you say and how you say it, what you do, and even what you wear. They notice if you're tired or well rested, if you're feeling dejected or upbeat, or if you're surly or joking. They learn your mannerisms, your weaknesses and strengths, your habits and routines, and your values. They also discuss you in terms of your professional capacity and what they've been able to cobble together about your personal life. They compare notes, trade juicy or telling anecdotes, and render judgments.

Living under a microscope can be a humbling and daunting experience, especially when your students have heard you "talk the talk" and are waiting to see if you're going to be able to "walk the talk."

No aspect of your behavior goes unnoticed. Living under a microscope can be a humbling and daunting experience, especially when your students have heard you "talk the talk" and are waiting to see if you're going to be able to "walk the talk." Values are the cornerstone of your curriculum and your discipline.

One subtlety about a classroom's activities is that teaching and learning aren't always directly linked. Students learn a whole range of behaviors in the classroom that may have nothing to do with whatever the teacher is teaching. A teacher may be instructing the class on the culture of Native Americans, but modelling the use of sarcasm, bullying, and perhaps even racism. In a very real sense, when you talk about values, you teach what you are.

The personal and the professional are inextricably linked. Teachers need to reflect regularly on their classroom behavior to discover, re-examine, and, if warranted, adjust the way their personal values affect their professional actions.

"Catching" Behavior

Never is the student spotlight on the teacher more intensely focused than during the first day and first week of school. For that reason, from the first bell teachers need to model the behavior and general deportment they expect from their students. Behavior is "caught" more than taught. And teachers set the tone.

Not only is it essential for teachers to be fair; they also have to be seen as fair. Students value and respect the concept of fairness above all others. Breaking faith with that concept leads to protest, resentment, and non-compliance.

Assigning class detentions, for instance, is a reaction to disruptive behavior that many teachers find irresistible and perfectly justified; students, however, see the practice as unfair. Some teachers will use the threat of a class detention when they perceive widespread misbehavior in the class or want to use peer pressure to modify the behavior of a few misbehaving students. Regardless of the reason, class

As you get to know each student's limits, don't expect more of individuals than you know they can handle.

detentions are never justified. Punishing the innocent undermines our basic understanding of justice in a democratic society.

Assigning class detentions also sends a signal to the class that the teacher can't identify or control those individuals who are non-compliant. The power dynamic in the classroom then shifts in their favor. Besides, the students who are most apt to behave disruptively are likely those who are least able to control their impulses. Threats and peer condemnation have little impact on the irresistible pressures motivating those who feel alienated in and persecuted or overwhelmed by institutional demands. Understanding the fairness doctrine requires teachers to look at whatever happens in the classroom from a student's perspective.

As you get to know each student's limits, don't expect more of individuals than you know they can handle. When individuals with self-control problems emerge, give them the same latitude as any other student. A handful of students are talking, for example, while the teacher delivers a lesson. The teacher views one of the students as constantly disruptive. The teacher might perceive this minor infraction as the final straw and punish the student for a series of behaviors; the student in question, however, is enraged to receive punishment far out of proportion to the behavior and, indeed, for being punished at all when other students are not. From the student's perspective, the teacher isn't being fair.

Similarly, be prepared to deal with disruptive behavior, but don't address the behavior pre-emptively. "While I'm teaching the lesson today, Robert, don't try to whisper behind my back." Although the teacher might feel justified in stifling disruptive behavior before it starts, the student feels singled out and publicly humiliated without justification. Look for that student to live *down* to the teacher's expectations at the earliest opportunity.

From the outset, as well, students have to be convinced that the rules of conduct exist for everyone in the classroom, especially the teacher. A double standard in that regard is an invitation to ignore those rules and mimic the negative model. For that reason alone, be sure to monitor and reflect on every remark you make.

As much as you introduce democratic principles into your classroom management techniques, you still have the absolute power to direct your students and they must acquiesce. Since this power imbalance exists, constantly reassure your students that you value them as individuals. Go out of your way to be courteous, using "please" and "thank you" at all times when interacting with them. Directions have a less dictatorial feel to them when softened with polite language. For example, when you say, "Stand up, please, Raymond," you achieve the desired effect while offering the student face-saving respect. In the same way, "Stop talking, please" and "Shut up" are similar directives with totally opposite connotations. You will also find that if you consistently avoid masculine pronouns when referring to mixed gender groups, students will also use "he or she" in their everyday speech. If teachers use inclusive language, students will pick it up and use it themselves; if teachers are polite and courteous with students, students will respond in kind.

When put-downs, sarcasm, and stereotyping come from teachers, though, students gain licence to indulge in similar behavior. A teacher's long, angry tirade may still a shocked and sullen class for a while, but the needless loss of control legitimizes negative behavior. Yelling condones yelling; bullying condones bullying. Angry confrontations promote resentment, heighten conflict, and seldom change behavior. Modelling positive values certainly won't be an instant cure; modifying and standardizing student behavior occurs slowly over time. But if teachers aren't consistent in their modelling or insist that students "do what I say not what I do," student behavior will never change.

Much learned behavior is already ingrained in students. What and how they've learned has been affected by experiences inside and outside the home and in past classrooms. It has also been affected by the great range and variety in their personalities, maturity levels, abilities, and learning exceptionalities. In most cases, this learned behavior works in the teacher's favor. Most students want to be well thought of and accepted by the teacher. They come to school ready to be instructed in the rules and routines and willing to abide by them. They expect to take part in interesting and stimulating activities and they want to get "good" grades. Other students, from their first day in Kindergarten, find adjustment to classrooms and school life difficult, even impossible. What and how they've learned has been dictated by emotional and psychological dysfunctions, severe learning disabilities, socio-economic inequities, and abuse of all kinds.

Although most students readily cope with and flourish under the artificial constraints and restraints of the classroom environment, some will be overwhelmed by the demands.

Although most students readily cope with and flourish under the artificial constraints and restraints of the classroom environment, some will be overwhelmed by the demands. Teachers must recognize and be prepared for the challenge of helping these troubled young people. Every classroom contains students who are difficult to serve. The students with the most serious problems will be identified and placed in special programs geared to accommodate their needs. Others will be identified and marked for accommodation in the regular classroom. Others still will struggle with classroom rules and routines, sometimes speaking and acting in inappropriate and disruptive ways, while the circumstances igniting their behavior remain undiagnosed. In the long term, teachers need to observe, investigate, and analyze the reasons behind negative and disruptive behavior. They need to address the causes rather than the symptoms. In the short term, however, such behavior must stop.

Every class is also different from every other class. Age, developmental factors, and experiential background are just some of the variables that make a Grade 2 class different from a Grade 3 class or a Grade 7 class different from a Grade 8 class. But two classes at the same grade level in the same school will often be far different from each other and different still from a class in another school. Even highly experienced teachers stand in front of their first classes on the first day and wonder what their students will be like.

Regardless of the character of any particular group of students, some individuals will soon begin to display resistance to and difficulty with the common rules and routines that regulate classroom life. You will need to identify and describe the pattern of behavior displayed by these individuals in an objective, specific, and dispassionate manner, at first with the student and possibly later with parents or school support personnel.

An observational checklist, such as that on page 30, will help you accumulate objective data about both the nature and the source of the student's difficulties. The checklist can also serve as the starting point in any discussion of the student's behavior and as a useful tool in assisting students to become aware of and to overcome their problematic behavior.

Observational Checklist

Student name _____

A. General Deportment

How frequently does the student . . .

	Never				Always
• accept individual differences?	1	2	3	4	5
• respect the rights of others?	1	2	3	4	5
• respect the property of others?	1	2	3	4	5
• respect other people's feelings?	1	2	3	4	5
• cooperate with others?	1	2	3	4	5
• become argumentative?	1	2	3	4	5
• display disruptive behavior?	1	2	3	4	5
• display aggressive behavior?	1	2	3	4	5
• assume responsibility for own actions?	1	2	3	4	5
• accept classroom/school rules?	1	2	3	4	5
• follow classroom/school routines?	1	2	3	4	5

B. Work Habits

How consistently does the student . . .

	Never				Always
• stay on task?	1	2	3	4	5
• complete in-class assignments?	1	2	3	4	5
• complete homework?	1	2	3	4	5
• seek help when necessary?	1	2	3	4	5
• display frustration?	1	2	3	4	5
• persevere?	1	2	3	4	5
• take risks (lack fear of making errors)	1	2	3	4	5
• try new things?	1	2	3	4	5

Talk, Talk, Talk

Teachers consistently underestimate how much talking they do and overestimate the amount of talking their students do.

The curriculum is language-based and talk-driven, but most of the talk has to come from the students. Students learn through talking. Although teachers understand that principle, they are also professional talkers. In studies comparing the amount of teacher-talk in a classroom to the amount of student-talk, the fact that teachers did most of the talking surprised no one — except the teachers. Teachers consistently underestimate how much talking they do and overestimate the amount of talking their students do. Regardless of the quantity, however, it's the quality of the talk that matters. What teachers don't underestimate is how much difficulty they have regulating student-talk. Primary, junior, and intermediate teachers complain about their students in the same way year after year:

- They're always talking; they never get down to work.
- They're always talking when I'm talking.
- They just blurt things out without putting up their hands.
- No matter how many times I tell them about their talking or how to answer in class, it doesn't seem to make a difference; it doesn't "stick."

After a while, teachers cast around for answers, eventually even questioning one another's competence: the Grade 3 teacher wonders about the Grade 2 teacher; the junior teachers wonder about the primary teachers; the intermediate teachers wonder about the junior teachers. They all wonder why no one has taught these students the basic rules about talking and answering in class or, if they have, why the years of reinforcement have had little impact.

Since talk is the foundation of learning in every classroom, the way in which talking behavior is structured determines how effectively learning can be conducted. From the first day in Kindergarten through every year of a student's school career, two fundamental rules are constantly intoned:

1. When the teacher asks for your attention, stop whatever you're doing or saying and attend.
2. One person at a time speaks during lessons. When you have something to say or an answer to give, raise your hand to be recognized. Never interrupt someone who is already speaking.

Some teachers add a third rule: Talking in the classroom is acceptable as long as students are talking about their schoolwork. Students adhere to this rule to the same degree that adults drive on the highway according to the posted speed limits. They know that enforcement won't begin until infractions become annoying and besides, since everyone else does it, they might as well try to get away with as much as they can.

Leaving the problematic third rule aside for the time being, ask yourself why the first two are so difficult to implement. If all teachers accept how critical talk management is to the creation of an efficient and effective learning/teaching environment, why don't students obediently do as they're told? Perhaps the answer lies in the fact that teachers and students don't view talking in the same way; perhaps students even live in a totally different world than adults do and have a whole set of different priorities.

By definition, students are egocentric. The younger they are, the more egocentric they are and the more they want *you* to know what's on their minds. Their heads are teeming with a chaotic sunburst of ideas, experiences, and feelings they need to share. A word or phrase from someone else will often spark such a jolt of recognition that they spontaneously blurt out their own association with that idea. Older students react in a similar fashion, but they've learned to monitor their output; the free association in their heads, although unspoken, is an ever-changing, private kaleidoscope of thoughts.

All students live intimate, intensely felt lives in which their personal, social, and physical concerns are of paramount importance. In their worlds, an object or incident outside a teacher's radar screen can trigger an emotional response that dwarfs into insignificance whatever the teacher is doing or saying.

Imagine yourself leading such an Alice-in-Wonderland existence. A new box of pencil crayons expands in importance to the size of an elephant in the classroom or the mere thought of the pack of trading cards in your pocket burns like a comet through the best of intentions to concentrate on that spelling list. The teacher doesn't know or care that you were called a name or that you just heard such a great joke that you're going to explode with laughter or that you're so hungry you can't think of anything but food. He or she is outside this subjective world.

As you grow older, the rift between this world and the teacher's continues. The teacher doesn't know or care about the way you were humiliated in gym class or the fact that you ate lunch alone again in a corner of the cafeteria. She or he is also unaware that the person you love is sitting two rows over and three seats down or that your former best friend is now spreading filthy rumors about you.

Along with these kinds of commonplace concerns, conflicts, and crises, try to imagine the content and state of a student's mind if the student has also suffered the trauma of abuse, neglect, or unbearable frustration. Now put all these students in front of you as the morning bell rings and wonder no longer why it's so hard to get their attention.

The problem worsens when inconsistencies in applying the rules undermine a teacher's efforts to limit talk in class. Students learn a lot about talking in the classroom from situations like these:

- The teacher constantly interrupts students as they answer, but chides students who interrupt each other.
- The teacher allows an interruption or interjection from a "star" pupil or a "difficult" student who seldom answers.
- The teacher says "We won't begin until everyone stops talking," but begins before everyone stops talking.
- The teacher has a double standard based on gender, that is, allowing one gender to transgress the rules and not the other.
- The teacher enforces the rules to different degrees from one period to another, from one day to another, or from one class to another.
- One teacher enforces the rules differently from another teacher in the same school.
- Rules in an assembly are enforced differently from those in a classroom.

Negative modelling plays a role in undermining the integrity of the basic rules about talking. Teachers can place a certain value on a learning situation, but undercut it by their own behavior. If students see teachers talking together in an assembly while the audience is supposed to be listening to a speaker, there is a dissonance. If students are instructed to attend to a special guest in the classroom, but the teacher sits at the back of the room marking, there is a dissonance. If

All students live intimate, intensely felt lives in which their personal, social, and physical concerns are of paramount importance.

students are reading silently, but the teacher is at the back of the room or out in the hallway conversing with a colleague or talking on a cell phone, there is a dissonance. Admittedly, teachers are busy multi-tasking and expedience often leads them to cut corners whenever they can. Negative modelling, however, has a price: teachers become complicit in encouraging the very behavior they don't want.

Students in a classroom, as you know, want to talk, and like pigeons, they inherently understand random reinforcement. Pigeons in a Skinnerian reward box will peck regularly at a food button if food appears every time they peck at the button. If food appears randomly and not every time they peck at the button, they are driven to peck incessantly. If students who attempt to bypass the basic rules about talking are randomly rewarded with success, they will test those rules incessantly. Once established, a negative behavior is extraordinarily difficult to extinguish.

Students might also discern and respond to inconsistencies in how teachers define a noisy classroom. An acceptable level of noise in the classroom varies from activity to activity, teacher to teacher, and school to school. When reading aloud or administering a written test, most teachers expect a quiet classroom; those same teachers anticipate a busy hum during small-group discussions, lab experiments, or group projects. Expectations become more individual and arbitrary when students are working on assignments at their desks. While some teachers encourage collaboration at all times, others treat seatwork as a test situation and demand absolute silence. The informal chatter that fills some classrooms before and in-between classes is never allowed in others. Schools with open space or shared teaching areas find an accommodation with noise that schools with single, closed classrooms never experience.

Complicating the issue further is the fact that many students are unaware of how loudly they talk; the younger the children, the less aware they will probably be. Some students simply have louder voices than others, and the issue of voice modulation needs to be recognized. Speak privately to students, encouraging them to make adjustments, giving them time and opportunity to improve, and making certain that you never embarrass them publicly.

Discipline Do's and Don'ts

Understanding student behavior is one thing; controlling student misbehavior is another. Just as conduct outside the school is circumscribed by regulations and conventions, student conduct inside the classroom must be governed by rules and routines. Once established, rules and routines allow students to function freely, yet within specific parameters. They must be easily understood, logical, purposeful, fair to all, and unswervingly applied. With young children or students of any age who find it hard to accept responsibility for their behavior, the language framing the rule or routine must be clear and direct. Keep in mind that, in most cases, students are already well versed in a school's code of conduct. Except for early primary classes, every class from day one will be familiar with the basic school rules.

During your first day with a class, employ a simple cooperative learning technique to develop rules specific to classroom behavior. Divide the class into groups of four to six students. Supply each group with chart paper and markers, and based on their own classroom experiences, ask them to articulate the five rules

If students who attempt to bypass the basic rules about talking are randomly rewarded with success, they will test those rules incessantly.

that everyone in the class should always observe. Give them a time limit of no more than twenty minutes. At the end of the prescribed time, collect the lists and tape them up on the walls, chalkboards, or display boards.

Direct the class to examine the lists and identify items common to most of the lists. One by one, discuss the pros and cons of adopting these rules to govern behavior in the current year. Some rules will appear on some lists and not others. Ask the groups suggesting these rules to justify their selection, and attempt to gain consensus on whether or not they should be adopted. As much as possible, retain the language originally used by the students, correcting and clarifying with their consent. When a group of rules has been adopted, ask a volunteer to rewrite them on chart paper and display them prominently in the classroom. When students transgress any of those rules, refer them to the list and use that language as a starting point for discussing the behavior.

Additional rules and routines governing classroom behavior are also best formulated in collaboration with students. Give your class or classes a week or two to become acclimatized to you and to one another; by that time, certain recurrent problems will begin to surface. When classes on rotary are changing classrooms, for example, the corridors may become clogged, resulting in much pushing and shoving. Perhaps a class is too noisy or disruptive going to or from the gymnasium, or maybe students are slow to attend when you need their attention or delay getting down to work on an assignment. Post the problems on the blackboard, explain why the behavior is untenable, and enlist the students' help in understanding and resolving the behaviors.

Small groups could again be used to address the problems. It is preferable to give each group a different behavior problem to discuss for five minutes as students who haven't examined a given problem themselves will listen more actively to group reports to the class as a whole. After every group report on causes, open the discussion to the whole class. When all situations have been thoroughly analyzed, send students back into their small groups to discover solutions. When they make their recommendations, solicit comments from the class as a whole again.

At the very least, with this technique, you've impressed on students what the problems are and why they need to be resolved. That understanding sets the groundwork for the reinforcement that will follow. Since the students have also been part of the solutions, they should more readily adopt whatever new routines or practices need to be introduced. Finally, no one knows more about why a certain kind of behavior occurs or what solutions may or may not be workable than students themselves. Get their expertise working for rather than against you.

Despite all the preparations you've made or the consensus you've established, some students will continue to display negative behavior. The range could go from mildly impolite to outrageously rude or from moderately distracting to unacceptably disruptive. The more you get to know all your students, the more prepared you'll be when you need to temper their actions. In all instances, however, your goal is to maintain and enhance the integrity of the learning/teaching atmosphere in your classroom.

When you begin a large-group lesson, for example, you can expect the emergence of a variety of common behaviors that prevent individuals from attending to the lesson. These behaviors also may distract you and others in the classroom. For example, students may talk, pass notes, complete homework from another class, draw cartoons, or just "goof around." Your objective should be to curtail the behavior without interrupting the flow of your lesson or the focus of your

No one knows more about why a certain kind of behavior occurs or what solutions may or may not be workable than students themselves.

class. Any harangue or emotional upset on your part defeats your purpose. Your actions will only add to the disruption, interfere with the lesson delivery, and impair the learning. If the student displaying the behavior is motivated by control or power issues, you will also reinforce the student's assumption of power by your own conspicuous reactions.

Instead, give the behavior the attention it deserves. Carry on with your lesson for the benefit of those who are attending and choose among these kinds of reactions:

Your objective should be to curtail the behavior without interrupting the flow of your lesson or the focus of your class. Any harangue or emotional upset on your part defeats your purpose.

- As you continue talking, don't move your gaze from face to face around the classroom. Simply stare at the offending student until he or she notices. Sometimes, just knowing that they've been spotted will deter some students.
- Mention the individual's name in the course of your lesson. For example: "The Native people, Margaret, were defenseless against alien diseases." People are especially sensitive to the sound of their own names. When the student looks up, you can smile and nod encouragingly, and not miss a beat.
- If the inattention resumes, casually walk over to the individual's desk as you teach and stand there for a moment or two. The student will get the message. With some students, you may have to sit on the edge of their desks for a few moments to set the habit of cooperation.
- In the case of individuals engaged in some kind of inappropriate reading, writing, or drawing, walk over to their desks as you continue talking and gently close the book or turn over the paper. Doing that allows you to interrupt the behavior without interrupting the lesson.
- Occasionally, you may have to stop talking and wait, merely staring at the offending student. When the student notices you've stopped and looks up, say something along the lines of "Thank you, Robert" and resume your lesson.

In the case of students who refuse to behave appropriately or who are unacceptably disruptive, you should consider removal from the classroom. If you try to deal with the situation in the classroom, you will get caught up in an escalating conflict and a struggle for control that will derail learning. In this case, quietly, politely, but firmly direct the student to wait for you in the hall outside the classroom door. You might say, "Michael, please wait in the hall outside the classroom door. I'll join you outside in a moment."

Refuse to engage the student in any kind of discussion. Repeat your instruction if necessary. If the student doesn't comply, explain that the student has two choices: to follow your instruction or to wait to be removed once you call the office. Again, refuse to engage the student in discussion. If the student doesn't comply, call the office. Even in this extreme situation, you've maintained control, offered the student a choice, resolved the conflict as calmly as possible, and sidelined whatever personal agenda the student might have.

Usually, however, the student will comply. As the student leaves, carry on with your lesson. At a convenient time, go outside and deal privately with the student. If at all possible, through leading questions, engage the student in naming the offending behavior, articulating the classroom expectations, and even suggesting consequences. To be fair, negotiate a time frame for compliance.

"Michael, why did I send you out here?"
"Why can't I allow that kind of behavior to continue?"

"What do I need to do to get you to change your behavior?"

"What do you think I should do if you don't change your behavior?"

"In tomorrow's class, if you can prove to me that you intend to cooperate, we'll wipe the slate clean and start fresh."

This concrete example illustrates the two main options available to teachers when dealing with inappropriate behavior: (1) to deal with the behavior inside the classroom; (2) to deal with the behavior outside the classroom. Each option has ramifications for both teacher and student.

As teachers prepare to respond to inappropriate behavior, but hope to restrict the disciplinary measures to the classroom, they should keep these questions uppermost in their minds:

- Will my actions stop the behavior without disrupting the learning atmosphere in the classroom?
- If I have to disrupt the learning atmosphere in the classroom, are my actions justified?
- Are my actions liable to cause or escalate conflict with this particular student? If the conflict flares dramatically, what measures might I be forced to take? How will my actions affect the student?

As teachers prepare to respond to inappropriate behavior, but intend to deal with it outside the classroom, they should realize they have a limited number of options.

As teachers prepare to respond to inappropriate behavior, but intend to deal with it outside the classroom, they should realize they have a limited number of options.

- They can deal with the student privately outside in the hallway.
- If necessary, especially if the student is reluctant to cooperate, they can continue the process privately after class or after school.
- They can make the situation public by sending the student to the office for disciplinary action by administration.
- They can make the situation public by informing the parents.

The last two options have serious consequences for the student.

Especially at the beginning of a school year, teachers are operating with little or no knowledge of the needs and problems of individual students. Fortunately, most students remain cooperative during those early days. As teachers notice particular students who seem reluctant to modify their behavior or who seem unusually disruptive, they have recourse to a number of support mechanisms. The goal, as always, is to identify why the student is behaving in this manner and how best to help the student modify the behavior and learn effectively. To throw added light on such behavior, teachers can consult some or all of the following:

- permanent student records;
- colleagues who also teach the student;
- teachers from the previous year;
- school guidance and administrative personnel;
- parents and guardians.

After these consultations, the student's behavior might be addressed in a parent-teacher conference with the student present. The teacher might also request consultation and assistance from psychological or other specialized support personnel.

Tactical Maneuvers

The universe can easily shrink to the confines of your classroom walls; discipline can degenerate into a soul-defeating "me" versus "them" solitude.

The universe can easily shrink to the confines of your classroom walls; discipline can degenerate into a soul-defeating "me" versus "them" solitude. Perspective is everything. Especially when trying to moderate, control, or even change student behavior, teachers have to keep a firm grip on their ultimate goals, anticipate the kinds of problems that might arise, and plan ahead for their optimum responses. The following set of reminders and suggestions should help teachers maintain their dispassionate objectivity and refine their practical techniques in the hurly-burly of the day-to-day classroom.

The rules of disengagement

In any conflict situation, the teacher has the mature perspective and judgment to define the situation and the power to defuse the conflict. Students who are ready to defy the teacher's authority have no objective perspective and are probably acting out of a deep sense of powerlessness and frustration. They are so wrapped up in their own conscious or unconscious agendas that they become trapped in an escalating power dynamic. If they back down, they are admitting that they were wrong and not wronged; if they back down, they lose face. Although it may not be possible at the time to identify why these students are acting as they are, the teacher can read the warning signs and realize that a lose-lose result has to be avoided. In these cases, the teacher has to find a way to disengage from and defuse the conflict.

If a student's reactions are unexpectedly vehement or out of proportion to the situation, you know that forces of which you are ignorant are at work. You can't negotiate in ignorance. When you see defiance building in a student's facial features, posture, or tone of voice, or hear belligerent or confrontational words, try to disengage.

Name the behavior in a disinterested manner and offer the student choices. For example: "I can see that you feel strongly about this matter and that you feel wronged. Let's take a break before we discuss it further. Maybe, you'd like a little 'time out' to go to the washroom or perhaps you'd like to tell your side to a guidance counsellor. You might want to think about why you're feeling so strongly and jot down some notes; that way you won't forget anything important. What's best for you to do right now?"

By questioning students and by always offering options, you never back them into a corner or force a confrontation. You also place the onus on the students to explain and justify their behavior.

Giving the benefit of the doubt

If you assume that students have valid reasons for their actions, you can't go wrong; assuming the opposite is a recipe for disaster. For instance, you see two students running in a hall ten minutes before the first bell. At this time, they shouldn't be in the school at all. Instead of bellowing accusations, call them over to you and ask them why they're in the hall and why they're in such a rush. They may be looking for help to break up a fight or assisting someone who's ill or chasing an intruder. Or, they may knowingly be in the wrong place at the wrong time.

In any event, checking first will save you from worlds of potential embarrassment and ensure that innocent students aren't punished.

The same tactic is invaluable in the classroom. Instead of admonishing a student for not getting down to work, mention that he or she seems to be having difficulty and offer to help. The student may be totally confused by the assignment and not know how to start, have lost the pertinent text, or may be upset about a situation you know nothing about. A sincere "How can I help you?" also works wonders for the procrastinating student who needs a gentle prod to get going.

Detention prevention

Detentions are usually a complete waste of time, especially the teacher's.

Detentions are usually a complete waste of time, especially the teacher's. The thinking seems to be: if you waste my time during class, I'll waste your time after class. If detentions curbed or changed behavior, you wouldn't see the same faces over and over after school or in the detention room. When a student has a detention with two or three other teachers on the same day and you are negotiating about when he or she can serve your detention, you begin to understand that to the student it's just a game. It's the price the student has to pay to continue doing whatever she or he wants to do. From a student point of view, a detention wipes the slate clean. Rather than deter behavior, detentions create a penal, "I've done my time" attitude.

Some teachers further confuse the issue by assigning "lines" from a dictionary. They demand that students write "I will not . . . (fill in the blank)" 500 times or complete an hour's worth of mathematical computations without a calculator. Not only is this kind of treatment mind-numbingly boring and purely punitive, the practice also guarantees that students will associate such purposeful activities as writing, using a reference text, or doing mathematical calculations with punishment. No wonder so many dictionaries gather dust, unused, on classroom shelves.

Detentions can be beneficial if approached as an opportunity to investigate a student's behavior and determine what might be done about it. Simply sitting down with a student and outlining how the student's behavior is affecting you and what you're trying to do can be a useful opening to an honest and fruitful discussion.

You might also want to use the time to have the student describe the inappropriate behavior in written form. The note, dated and signed by the student, can be placed in your files as part of the record of the student's deportment over time. When you need to appeal to parents or administration for assistance in helping the student, such records are persuasive evidence.

Behavior contracts

Detentions can also be used to pursue behavior contracts. A contract is a written agreement with a student to formalize a change process. Contracts can be introduced to modify a variety of behaviors from systematizing work and study habits to curbing inappropriate conduct. They are only effective, however, if students first recognize the need to change. Before approaching a student about implementing a contract, you would be wise to document the behavior that needs to be changed. Documented observations offer students a concrete picture of their actions over time and an objective starting point for a discussion on modifying their behavior.

The following sample documentation illustrates both points:

Student: Brandon Winters

Date	Observation	Action Taken
Sept. 23	• hmwrk not done	• check tomorrow
Sept. 24	• hmwrk still not done	• complete after school
Sept. 26	• difficulty concentrating on in-class assignment	• discussed situation; understands concepts
Sept. 27	• yesterday's assignment not completed	• complete after school
Oct. 5	• hmwrk carelessly done	• says I'm "picking on him"
Oct. 6	• yesterday's assignment incomplete	• belligerent when confronted

With this kind of documentation, students will readily recognize the need to alter their approach. Once they do, the discussion can move on to setting a clear, attainable goal within a specified period of time. Start with a small modification within a narrow time frame; early success will fuel the next modification. Agree, as well, on the observable evidence that will constitute improvement and signify reaching the stated goal. The contract is then written up, signed by the student, and copies retained by the student and the teacher.

Behavior Contract

Student: *Brandon Winters*

Date: *Oct. 6*

Terms: *Brandon pledges to faithfully and thoughtfully complete all class and homework assignments from his Science classes for the period from Oct. 7 to Oct. 13. On Oct. 14, he will present his work for that period for inspection.*

Student signature: *Brandon Winters*

Teacher witness: *J. Furlough*

The following section to be completed on *Oct. 14*

Start with a small modification within a narrow time frame; early success will fuel the next modification.

At the end of the designated time period, the contract forms the basis of another meeting with the student to evaluate progress. If the student has met the conditions of the contract, teacher and student decide whether to extend the same contract to consolidate the progress, set a new goal with a new contract, or allow the student to assume responsibility for continued improvement without a contract.

If the conditions of the contract haven't been met, the teacher must decide whether a second contract is a viable option or whether the guidance counsellors, school administrators, and/or parents should be involved. If others are brought into the process, the earlier observations and the unfulfilled contract will provide them with a clear window into the nature of the problem.

A photocopiable version of a behavior contract appears as an appendix.

Routine interceptions

When you confine thirty or more young people to a relatively small enclosure, you are bound to have problems; the longer they're confined, the more probable the problems. How are washroom and water fountain breaks to be regulated? How do students ask for assistance or materials? What restrictions, if any, should be placed on their movements within the classroom, such as to pencil sharpeners, waste baskets, reference texts, or a friend at the back of the room? What do you do if they need to go to their lockers for a text, or make a phone call home for their homework, or see another teacher about a lost assignment due five minutes ago?

Any time students enter the classroom is also problematic. How much of their "stuff" — knapsacks, caps, jackets, binders, texts, supplies, water bottles, and such — should they bring with them? Where do they put their "stuff" when they come in? All the interests, enthusiasms, passions, problems, and concerns that infused their lives before they entered the classroom come with them. How do you get them to settle down and focus on your current teaching priority?

Most schools on a rotary system have set routines for dealing with such issues as when students may go to lockers, what they should carry with them, when they can use the telephones, and how they can move around the school. In these schools, teachers often have considerable latitude with their own classroom routines. Classrooms on a limited rotary schedule or none at all often leave routines entirely to the discretion of the individual teachers. In either case, the more that teachers consult with one another and systematize their approaches, the better for all concerned. Invariable, consistently applied routines enable students to anticipate and adapt to changing environments either from classroom to classroom or from year to year.

In general, the best routines are as simple and serviceable as possible. If you're constantly recognizing a forest of hands with requests to go to the washroom, get a drink of water, or borrow a ruler, your routines are failing you. If you don't allow your students to go to the washroom, get a drink, or borrow a ruler, you're failing your students. Instead, find a routine that removes the decision making from your shoulders, yet regulates who gets to go where and when.

Except for early primary children, institute a clipboard record on which students note when they leave or re-enter the classroom. The photocopied sheets contain the date, a place for names, destination, time leaving, and time returning. Decide how many students may leave at any one time — one person to get a drink

Find a routine that removes the decision making from your shoulders, yet regulates who gets to go where and when.

and one to go to the washroom is a popular choice — and inform your students that they should leave only under those conditions.

If they haven't encountered this routine before, students will initially turn the classroom door into a revolving turnstile — the built-in independence is irresistible. When the novelty wears off, however, few abuse the privilege and the routine operates effectively and independently.

Place the clipboard somewhere in the classroom where you can keep an eye on it. You needn't arrange for a student to monitor clipboard use. Turning students into the "washroom" police merely creates an unneeded and unpredictable complication. However, you can use the written record as a basis to discuss with students who seem to be leaving too often whether or not they have a problem with which you can help.

Sitting on a hard, plastic chair for forty to eighty or more minutes at a time is an endurance test. Encouraging students to move around now and then solves several problems, including the need to stretch their legs. They shouldn't need to ask permission to recycle paper, sharpen a pencil, or get a dictionary: a classroom should operate more like an office than a prison. By the same token, pencils break all the time and the pencil sharpener makes an annoying sound. Some teachers keep a can of sharpened pencils on their desks to solve that dilemma; students can exchange a blunt pencil for a sharpened one at any time.

Be prepared for students who forget their tools, too. Students are always forgetting to bring pencils, pens, erasers, or rulers to class; they always will, notwithstanding reminders, lectures, admonitions, and warnings. Keeping a few of each tool on your desk for their use is always appreciated, and most will be returned at the end of the period. Adding the inadvertently discarded pens, pencils, and erasers on the classroom floor at the end of the day replenishes your supplies. When you run out, "pass the can" around the classroom and ask for donations. You'll be pleasantly surprised at the results.

Nothing in teaching is more essential or problematic than securing attention at a moment's notice. Teacher folklore is a font of sure-fire methods for doing just that; unfortunately, while each technique may work for some classes some of the time, none of them works for all classes all of the time. The following list features a few of these practices ranging from the ingenious to the desperate:

Nothing in teaching is more essential or problematic than securing attention at a moment's notice.

- Flick the classroom lights off and on.
- Play music as students enter the classroom and turn it off when you want attention.
- Clap your hands.
- Stand at the front of the class and stare silently for as long as it takes for the students to attend.
- Talk at a whisper until curiosity works its magic.
- Start talking and refuse to repeat yourself if some students can't hear.
- Threaten the class with a class detention if all students don't pay attention this minute.
- Pick out students who won't pay attention and write their names on the board for a detention after school.
- Pick out students who are talking and ask them to stand up until the talking dwindles off and they all sit down again.
- Yell "Shut up!" as loudly as you can while banging your head against the chalkboard.

All these techniques have been devised to solve the same problem. It usually takes about five minutes for all your students to enter the class and sit down. By the time the last stragglers have wandered in, those who came in earlier have become preoccupied with their own conversations or with tasks totally unrelated to whatever you have for them to do. Inevitably, you find yourself forced to shout them down before you can even begin your lesson. If you encounter resistance or defiance in the process, the learning atmosphere readily turns sour.

A simple routine goes to the source of the problem. If students enter the classroom already knowing they have an assignment to begin, you don't need to gain their attention as a group. You don't need to talk to the group at all. Whether it's completing a journal entry, solving a set of mathematical problems, setting up an experiment, or simply reading a section from a text, students can get on with the task at hand. The same activity can start every period every day or a new start-up assignment can be placed on the chalkboard prior to the beginning of the class. This routine operates most effectively when the initial assignment is integrated into the content of the lesson. The reading assignment is based on the theme of the day's history lesson, for example, or the mathematical problems either review the previously taught concept or introduce a new concept.

Make your expectations clear and make no exceptions. With most of the class already focused and engaged, you can approach individuals to enquire about why they haven't begun the assignment. Try to be helpful, not confrontational; however, if the student has no valid reason for procrastinating or avoiding the task, insist that the student follow your directions. Once everyone is "on task," it's relatively easy to gain the group's attention and begin your lesson.

Admitting the human factor

Managing thirty or more students at any one time is a monumental task for anyone. You are inevitably going to act impatiently, impulsively, or rashly; sometimes, you'll yell, lose your temper, and generally make poor choices. Expect that you'll make mistakes and be prepared to deal with them. If you're feeling harried or stressed, sick, or just out of sorts, for instance, let your students know. Forewarned, they'll be more likely to "tread lightly" that day or attribute your behavior to the way you're feeling.

Don't be afraid to apologize for your mistakes.

Don't be afraid to apologize for your mistakes. Some teachers maintain the allusion that they need to be or at least appear to be perfect. They view apologizing as a sign of weakness and vulnerability. The opposite is true, however. Your students know only too well how imperfect you are; remember that you've been under their microscopes since they first met you. They expect you to make mistakes; they may not be expecting you to apologize.

When you do or say the wrong thing at the wrong time to the wrong student, admit it. When you inadvertently hurt someone's feelings, own up to it. Sometimes, a private word with a student explaining why you acted the way you did and what you were trying to accomplish will be enough. Sometimes, you'll need to admit to your whole class that you've hurt someone's feelings and that you'll try to handle a similar situation differently next time it arises. An honest apology will not only heal the hurt you've caused in the individual, but also earn you respect from all your students. With one simple act, you've provided a model for the kind of behavior you expect from your students and reaffirmed the basic values that underpin your classroom.

Dealing with Control Disorders

The comprehensive behavioral framework you've established is even more important for students who may be unable to consistently control or regulate their behavior. An estimated 8 to 10 percent of students are affected by control disorders that will impede their own progress and hurt the learning/teaching atmosphere of the classroom as a whole. As well as having clinical behavioral problems that usually emerge well before puberty, these students are also often afflicted with one or more learning or attention deficit disabilities. In general, these students will be impulsive, inattentive, or hyperactive; depending on their condition, they are prone to angry outbursts, sometimes leading to acts of violence.

Identifying specific disorders can be difficult.

Students suffering from ODD (Oppositional Defiant Disorder), for instance, may also be affected by an attention deficit disorder or possess one or more learning disabilities. These students will seek out confrontation with the teacher and act in a defiant, hostile, and disobedient manner.

Students suffering from CD (Conduct Disorder) will also appear tough and hostile. These students frequently disobey rules, initiate aggressive behavior, and even destroy property, alone or in the company of a gang. In spite of their obvious and constant inappropriate and dangerous behavior, they tend to blame others for their actions and display little understanding of or sympathy for other people's rights and feelings. Poor literacy skills often compound their sense of alienation in and frustration with the classroom environment.

The behavior strategies that guide and benefit students in general are similar to the strategies needed for students suffering behavior disorders.

Teachers should view the conduct of all these students as symptomatic of a disorder rather than as volitional misbehavior. At the same time, they should never accept or condone the negative behavior. Fortunately, the behavior strategies that guide and benefit students in general are similar to the strategies needed for students suffering behavior disorders. The following strategies should be in place for the first class in September:

- Develop explicit expectations, rules, and boundaries for the whole class in collaboration with the students. Ensure that these are expressed in plain language that everyone understands. Post them in the class. Refer to them when defining unacceptable behavior.
- Insist that all students meet the expectations and observe the rules and boundaries. Be consistent.
- Individualize your program to match the needs of students with learning disabilities.
- Document repeated and significant cases of non-compliance. Some students have difficulty seeing patterns in their behavior and benefit from reviewing their immediate history. Parents, guidance counsellors, administrators, and other support personnel will require documentation to understand the parameters of the problem and how to assist with solutions.
- Notice, mention, and praise compliant behavior.
- Ensure that consequences follow non-compliant behavior. Consequences, however, must suit the behavior and have the goal of encouraging compliance. In some cases, a consequence might entail the teacher sitting down with the student to ensure that the student understands the unacceptable nature

of the behavior. In other cases, the teacher might suggest options for a student who is feeling extreme frustration or anger.

- Establish an acceptable routine for angry or troubled students to remove themselves from the classroom environment and find immediate assistance or a place to cool off or calm down. Some teachers post a time-out pass near the classroom door. The students are briefed beforehand to use the pass when needed and where to go when they leave the classroom. A guidance room, a bench beside the main office, or a nurse's office could serve the purpose. The classroom teacher must always notify guidance or administrative personnel when a student leaves the classroom on time out to ensure that the student is carefully monitored.

Students suffering from ADD (Attention Deficit Disorder) exhibit a variety of symptoms. These students will have difficulty listening at length, following directions, or concentrating on a task. They will appear disorganized and display a puzzling inconsistency in effort and ability; one day they will be able to accomplish a specific task and the next day they won't. They also may be hyperactive, unable to remain seated or in one place for long or to wait their turn. Students with ADD often become frustrated easily, tend to speak out unthinkingly, and seem socially immature. Learning disabilities and low self-esteem frequently accompany their condition.

In addition to the general measures already in place for guiding and shaping behavior, the following strategies are recommended for students with ADD:

- Seek expert help from guidance counsellors, administrators, and support personnel.
- Collaborate with parents or guardians to learn about a student's history and specific approaches that have worked in the past.
- Motivate with praise and positive reinforcement.
- Provide the students with feedback on what you observe them doing and how they appear to others.
- Ask the students to tell you what kind of assistance they feel would help them.
- Supply them with checklists, schedules, and reminders to bolster their organization.
- Keep instructions to them brief and to the point and be willing to repeat them.
- Reinforce your time-out routine to provide them with a safety valve.

Understanding Bullying

Teachers can make a difference, but must first understand the behavior of both bully and victim.

Bullying cuts across all ages and genders and is found in all schools. The main difficulty with bullying in schools lies not in what to do about it, but rather in recognizing its serious and all-pervasive nature. Since the behavior involves conflict among students, occurs most often outside the classroom, and is rarely reported by victims, teachers may be unaware of its severity and frequency. Teachers can make a difference, but must first understand the behavior of both bully and victim. They can then search for the signs of bullying in classrooms, change rooms, hallways, yards, and cafeterias. When they do uncover bullying, teachers must consistently and unequivocally intervene.

Developmental psychologist Gordon Neufeld asserts that attachment is the most powerful force in human behavior, pointing out that a large portion of the emotional functioning of the human brain is devoted to preserving our emotional attachments. According to his theory, both bullies and their victims lack this essential, emotional link with adults: for one, it becomes the source of their anger; for the other, the paradoxical need for acceptance from the very group ostracizing them. Bullies very clearly recognize the vulnerability and dependency of their victims since they have insulated themselves against their own need for love and acceptance.

Bullies become emboldened if they sense that a potential target is vulnerable.

While this theory sheds light on the dynamics in some extreme types of bullying, it fails to recognize or explain the diversity found in bully-target behavior. Targets for harassment can be chosen for any number of reasons. They aren't necessarily victims nor do they necessarily seek or need acceptance from the bully's peer group. Simply being a newcomer to a school without immediate friends or alliances might be enough to draw a bully's attention. A perceived slight, a manner of dress or deportment, association with a disliked peer or relative, or even success in school could be reason enough for one person to bully another. On the other hand, bullies become emboldened if they sense that a potential target is vulnerable.

Targets are perceived as vulnerable for a variety of reasons: social or physical ineptness, physical or psychological disability, sexual orientation, and ethnocultural or socio-economic inequity can drive a wedge between individuals and their peer groups. A bully can further alienate a target by forestalling a sympathetic backlash from the dominant student culture. Anyone in the peer group defending a vulnerable individual invites scorn by association. Someone defending a target labelled "gay," for example, will be themselves labelled "gay." According to a Toronto District School Board survey, "gay" is one of the first words that English as a Second Language students learn.

Bullying is difficult to ferret out. Bullies are careful to shield their behavior from adults and use threats and intimidation to silence their victims. When confronted, they claim they were only "kidding" or "fooling around." They might even accuse their victims of first victimizing them.

Harassment is endemic and escalates through students' school years. Although primary students "tell" on one another all the time, as students move through the junior grades and beyond, they are more aware of the consequences of reporting. These include being beaten up, being rejected, and losing the respect of friends.

Even when offered protection from retaliation, victims are still reluctant to admit their harassment or name their harassers, if recognized. Simply "ratting" on another student breaks the code of social solidarity against the adult world and invites further and more widespread ostracism, ridicule, and harassment.

This adolescent code of silence is especially strong when boys bully girls. Boys expect social sanction for "teasing," a form of relationship aggression that amounts to sexual harassment. They will throw their arms around a girl's neck at will, make sexually explicit comments or jokes, use sexual slurs, such as "bitch" or "slut," or spread unwarranted rumors. Girls are expected to endure this kind of hazing, resisting and responding in a mild way if necessary. In one survey, 80 percent of high school girls reported they had been harassed. If girls complain to a teacher about this kind of behavior, they risk scorn and retribution from both the boys and girls in their peer group. The teacher will also be assured by the onlookers that the boys didn't "mean anything" by their behavior.

By definition, ethnocultural or religious minorities are always at risk of bullying. These students can find themselves scorned for the color of their skin, their lack of English fluency, their lack of knowledge about sports or other recreational activities, for the way they dress, what they eat, how they spend their free time, or for what they believe. If they have other physical, psychological, socio-economic, or sexual differences as well, they become even more vulnerable to harassment. Regardless of perceived differences, a Toronto District School Board survey, for one, found that the word "fag" was the most common put-down.

Complicating the issue even more, victims or potential victims will sometimes bully others in an attempt to avoid being targeted or ostracized themselves. Students who are homosexual can become rabidly homophobic, an immigrant fluent in English will scorn other immigrants lacking such fluency, or someone inept at sports will mock another student with a stutter. Many students are constantly in a struggle to define and defend their place in the peer group pecking order. Put-downs, slurs, jibes, and innuendos of all kinds are never purposeless or harmless: on the slippery slope of social acceptance, some students are fighting to maintain a toehold while others scheme to push the vulnerable to the bottom.

Becoming Aware of Relationship Aggression

A double standard based on gender has always complicated how teachers regard and react to bullying. It still does. Culturally, teachers believe that girls tend to behave well while boys are bound to misbehave. They still have difficulty believing that female students can be physically aggressive. The "sugar and spice" image also creates a subconscious barrier to recognizing the endemic psychological and emotional bullying that permeates female peer groups.

With girls, popularity, valued over independence and competence, is power.

Although physical aggression is not uncommon, the customary tools of female aggression are rumor, gossip, scorn, and ostracization directed at their own gender. Boys derive their social power from a number of sources, including physical prowess and courage — a loner with perceived attributes can be admired, for example, by other boys and by girls. With girls, though, popularity, valued over independence and competence, is power. Since friends determine popularity, withdrawal of friendship is equated with alienation. Especially during junior high and high school years, cliques rule.

Friendship bonds between and among girls are crucial to their lives; with friendship comes strength and support in the battle to maintain individual self-esteem and even safety against the threat and power of the "in crowd." The more friends you have and the more popular you appear, the more attractive you become as a friend to others. The reverse, unfortunately, is also true.

Popularity is most often derived from some interpretation of the beauty myth, a term popularized by Naomi Wolf, who wrote *The Beauty Myth.* A young female who is acknowledged as more beautiful, more fashionable, more socially knowledgeable and adept, or more skillful at manipulating males is perceived as more powerful and more popular. In some cases, athleticism, along with one or more of the other "desirable" traits, can imbue an individual with popularity. Being a member of that person's clique, even as a hanger-on, makes any individual feel accepted and worthwhile; rejection from the group is ostracism and exile.

The signposts in relationship aggression may be subtle or overt. Teachers should be on the alert for abrupt changes in an individual's mood, signs of upset and distress, individuals who are isolated or seem fearful, hostilities among groups of friends, or heightened emotions and angry language. A rumor, for instance, is a serious and sometimes cataclysmic event in an individual's life. Teachers not only have to be ready to intervene in such situations, but also to expend much effort in tracking down "who said what to whom and why." Without a teacher's sincere and understanding mediation, aggression and victimization will proceed unabated.

The Need to Monitor Student Behavior

Although differences in gender bullying can be generalized, they aren't carved in stone. Relationship aggression can be discovered in the way boys deal with boys, and physical aggression can be a facet of girls dealing with girls. Bullying is just another example of both boys and girls being capable of unacceptable behavior. To be effective in routing out and controlling bullying, teachers must first accept responsibility for supervising and maintaining the well-being of all their students. They have to pursue the signs of misbehavior within and without the classroom walls; they also have to accept the necessity for examining and intervening in the personal lives of their students.

Everything that happens in and around a school is the teacher's province.

Everything that happens in and around a school is the teacher's province. In the discipline maze, the academic, personal, and social paths mix and merge in complicated and unexpected ways. Disentangling the intricacies of behavior requires patience and commitment. To be effective disciplinarians, teachers have to recognize what's going on, treat the events and mores of a young person's world seriously and with respect, and find solutions for misbehaving young people who can't find them on their own.

3

The Evaluation Merry-go-round

"The curriculum is so crowded that I barely have time to teach and test one concept before I have to move on to the next ."
"What's wrong with using objective-style testing?"
"What are the fastest, easiest, and best ways to evaluate?"
"We teach; we test. It's not complicated!"

We teach; we test. Nothing could be simpler, except that nothing about evaluation is or should be that simple. Your evaluation system needs to be as wide-ranging and meaningful as your program and as flexible, varied, and imaginative as your means to deliver that program. Evaluation and curriculum, in fact, are the yin and yang of education. In *Language Development: Kindergarten Through Grade Twelve*, Walter Loban tellingly defined this interdependence when he declared, "The curriculum inevitably shrinks to the boundaries of evaluation; if your evaluation is narrow and mechanical, that is what your curriculum will be."

We've been too conditioned to thinking of evaluation as an end point in the learning process. We test at the end of a unit, at the end of a term, or at the end of a year; if we test at any other time, it's usually with some kind of standardized test to assess the cumulative learning that has already taken place. When we prepare our lessons, evaluation is generally the last element we devise; if we read a book about educational methodology, evaluation is usually the last chapter.

That kind of thinking about evaluation has to be turned around. Evaluation isn't something you do after the learning; it's something you do before the learning takes place.

Learning is a purposeful activity: we learn to make sense of and to cope with our lives. In the same way, evaluation is a purposeful activity: we evaluate to make sense of and cope with our learning. Evaluation is the engine that powers learning and learning, the fuel that feeds the engine. If an evaluation system doesn't fit this dynamic definition, it will inevitably impede and stunt learning. If evaluation isn't the driving force within a recursive learning process, it can act only as a roadblock on a single-lane highway.

In the hurly-burly of daily testing and marking, however, teachers are so lost in the trees that they often lose sight of the forest. We teach; we test. The practical

Evaluation isn't something you do after the learning; it's something you do before the learning takes place.

imperatives of maintaining a prescribed course and reporting schedules keep us so intently focused on the what and when of evaluation that we're left with little room for exploring the why and how. Trapped on an evaluation merry-go-round, we never seem to have the time to reflect on or question why we evaluate the way we do — we just do it.

Practice over time produces a rough-knit, pragmatic approach to evaluation that, taken as a whole, produces a de facto, personal philosophy. How we conduct the day-to-day business of evaluation, as a result, says a lot about how we believe evaluation should operate.

The questionnaire on page 50 will help you examine your evaluation practices with a view to better understanding your beliefs.

After completing the questionnaire, you might find it interesting to go back over the items and reflect on your usual practices. What does the questionnaire tell you about your beliefs when you ignore certain approaches, for example, or regularly adopt others? Which techniques would you like to use more often and which should you use less? What concepts evolving out of the questionnaire items would you like to learn more about? How valid are some of your practices and why is it so hard to implement other approaches?

The intent of this questionnaire is formative: you can use it as a basis for discussion of the relative merits of various practices, as a diagnostic tool for personal needs and growth, or as a window into your personal beliefs about evaluation. You are in control of the results and how they're used.

The same questionnaire, however, can be transformed into a summative instrument by changing the intent. If each item in the questionnaire was identified as either a "recommended" or a "questionable" practice and marks assigned for correct, partially correct, or incorrect answers, the scores could be used to make judgments about an individual's evaluation practices. In this case, an evaluator, not the reader, would be in control of the results and how they are used.

Trapped on an evaluation merry-go-round, we never seem to have the time to reflect on or question why we evaluate the way we do — we just do it.

Evaluating Your Evaluation

How often do you	Never	Sometimes	Regularly
• give a test and **not** record the marks for report card purposes?	❏	❏	❏
• use rewards, such as stickers, candies, money, free time, "fun" activities, to acknowledge achievement?	❏	❏	❏
• use the same test you used in a previous year?	❏	❏	❏
• give a retest if students would like to improve their marks?	❏	❏	❏
• set a test or exam at the same time as you plan your unit?	❏	❏	❏
• match the type of testing you do (performance, essay, T or F, etc.) with the objectives for the learning?	❏	❏	❏
• record your observations and use them as part of your total assessment?	❏	❏	❏
• "weight" marks from a particular test (assign a percentage in relation to their importance to the learning)?	❏	❏	❏
• use a computer recording program that converts all marks to percentages and keeps a running total?	❏	❏	❏
• employ a diagnostic test to discover what students already know?	❏	❏	❏
• employ a diagnostic test to determine what you should teach?	❏	❏	❏
• use commercially prepared tests that accompany learning materials?	❏	❏	❏
• use easy-to-mark tests to save time?	❏	❏	❏
• have students mark their own work?	❏	❏	❏
• have students mark other students' work?	❏	❏	❏
• discuss test or exam results with all students on an individual basis?	❏	❏	❏
• discuss test or exam results with some students on an individual basis?	❏	❏	❏
• discuss test or exam results with all students as a class group?	❏	❏	❏
• use performance testing (that is, students perform a task rather than answer questions or write about it)?	❏	❏	❏
• employ group evaluations (e.g., all members of a group project receive the same mark)?	❏	❏	❏
• employ formative self-evaluation, or assessment aimed at assisting learning and personal growth?	❏	❏	❏
• employ summative self-evaluation, where marks are counted for report card purposes?	❏	❏	❏
• employ formative peer-evaluation (e.g., marks **aren't** counted for report card purposes)?	❏	❏	❏
• employ summative peer-evaluation (e.g., marks **are** counted for report card purposes)?	❏	❏	❏

Identifying Your Intentions

Teachers are necessarily focused on the prescribed elements of student evaluation — they have to be. Many school boards have implemented standardized testing at multiple grade levels. They've also mandated the number of reporting periods and even the curriculum criteria or learning strands that must be evaluated on each of the report cards to parents. Teachers are so squeezed by the short intervals between report cards and so pressured to generate marks to justify their summative assessments that they often neglect formative evaluation. Formative evaluation, however, lies at the heart of the learning process.

The difference between the two types of evaluation becomes clear in the following chart:

Formative evaluation	Summative evaluation
• focused on daily, ongoing assessment of student progress • focused on daily, ongoing assessment of program effectiveness • incorporates a diagnostic function for both student and program • geared to individual needs and growth • intended to assist students in learning • intended to improve educational experience • assumes teacher acting as trusted adult partner	• utilizes records for report card purposes • uses comparative standards and judgments • intended for overall decision-making, for example, student placement in a specific program or grade • assumes teacher acting as adult/evaluator

The evaluation system must be transparent.

The tension between the endless demand on teachers for accountability on the one hand and the intrinsic needs of the learners on the other has to be resolved. When formative evaluation is ignored, students quickly realize that everything they do in class — every piece of work the teacher looks at, and every test they take — "counts" toward the grade that ends up on their report card. In that kind of environment, concepts at the core of learning, such as risk taking, the benefits of trial and error, revision, collaboration, program modification, self-evaluation, and personal growth, are undercut, devalued, and aberrated. For the learning/teaching environment to operate effectively and rationally, a compromise has to be struck between formative and summative evaluation.

Fortunately, although the intent of formative and summative evaluation is different, summative evaluation can have an essential formative outcome. The key lies in defining and declaring clear and specific learning objectives to the students before the learning takes place. The evaluation system must be transparent. Right from the start, students should know not only what they will be learning, but also how and when they will be evaluated. If students know precisely the criteria by which they will be evaluated — even down to the number of marks assigned to specific skills or concepts — they will more readily direct their efforts to meeting those criteria.

As a concrete illustration of how this mechanism operates, look at page 53 and consider the rubric for evaluating small-group discussion skills. Imagine the impact on a group of students when they receive this marks sheet before they've even been exposed to a small-group experience or been instructed in the specific skills required for effective discussion. They will look at the discrete items and the assigned marks and understand immediately the behaviors that will be rewarded. The rubric is transformed into a road map for succcess.

This approach to summative evaluation becomes even more powerful when students have the opportunity to set some of the criteria themselves and assume ownership for the direction of their own learning. For students to take an active role in the learning process, they need to see evaluation as a tool and to feel they have control over its use. In the case of the small-group discussion rubric, for example, students might question how much active talking is rewarded and request a change in the weighting of the marks. If the teacher agrees to increase the marks for supporting behaviors in discussions, for instance, the class will be strongly motivated to practise those behaviors.

Some teachers slavishly follow a pretest-teach-posttest protocol. In this model, they hope to establish in the students' minds the goals for the planned learning and a baseline for comparison after the learning event has occurred. But testing prior to any planned learning event is only part of the answer; the intent of and context around a pretest determine the extent and effectiveness of its role in energizing learning. If a teacher uses the marks from a pretest in a summative manner or counts the posttest score in isolation rather than in comparison with the pretest score, for example, the benefits of pretesting are lost.

The pretest-teach-posttest model, however, has potential for enhancing the learning/teaching environment in several ways. A teacher may use a pretest, for instance, to ascertain what elements of a prescribed curriculum to emphasize in the teaching to follow; the results from that same pretest can be compared to the results on a posttest to measure the learning that has occurred and to assess the effectiveness of the instruction. Since the pretest offers a glimpse of the goals of the coming instruction, as previously mentioned, it can definitely indirectly influence the behavior of individual learners. If the specific criteria for evaluating the learning are added to the pre-learning preparation, however, a pretest can empower learners. Intent again plays a crucial role in this kind of empowerment.

The intent of the evaluation system directly influences the perception of the learners. If students perceive evaluation only as a series of grades that are totalled and placed on a report card, the curriculum is in trouble. Evaluation has a profound impact on all aspects of the learning/teaching environment. If the objectives of the program stress the development of higher thinking skills, for example, but the evaluation system emphasizes mainly factual recall, students will conclude that the learning of facts is the goal of the program. Similarly, if the classroom program stresses the acquisition of process skills, but the evaluation system assesses only the products of that process, students will short-circuit the process.

Designing an evaluation system that supports and stimulates learning is a complex and demanding task. There are so many interdependent facets and variables that no one gets it right all the time. Add in the external factors and pressures that classroom teaching is heir to and the frustrations with evaluation, at times,

The intent of the evaluation system directly influences the perception of the learners.

Summative Evaluation Marks Sheet for Small-Group Discussion Skills

Degree to which the student **shares** with others in a group by

- freely offering opinions, feelings, or special knowledge;
- listening carefully to know what to add to the discussion and when;
- giving facts and reasons to support opinions.

/ 10

Degree to which the student **replies** effectively to others in a group by

- listening carefully to be able to ask clarifying questions or make clarifying statements;
- responding freely to other people's questions, interests, problems, and concerns;
- sharing equally in the talking.

/ 10

Degree to which the student **shows leadership** in a group by

- suggesting own ideas, other ways to solve problems, or new directions for the group to explore;
- speaking up without cutting someone off or interfering with the progress the group is making;
- offering suggestions without dominating the discussion.

/ 10

Degree to which the student **supports** others in a group by

- helping another person have his or her turn to speak;
- speaking up without cutting off another person or too abruptly changing the subject;
- indicating interest in what is being said using gestures, facial expressions, or posture;
- giving people credit when they deserve it.

/ 10

Degree to which the student **evaluates** a group's progress by

- indicating agreement or disagreement with ideas and decisions and reasons for taking that position;
- considering how well the group is working and finding ways to help the group work even more effectively;
- re-examining own opinions and decisions and adjusting them when someone comes up with better ideas.

/ 10

Total   / 50

can seem insurmountable. If your evaluation system encompasses most of the following principles, you're doing wonders with a thorny and tangled challenge.

In general, a comprehensive evaluation system should encompass the following objectives:

- derive from, reflect, and stimulate specific learning behaviors
- assess both process and product
- address both affective and cognitive behaviors
- match the method of evaluation with the nature of the learning objective (e.g., a performance objective should be evaluated through performance)
- contain both formative and summative components
- include self- and peer-evaluation elements in formative evaluation
- include self-evaluation as a component of summative evaluation when students have developed the requisite experience and skills
- acknowledge self-evaluation as the eventual goal of all evaluation
- be flexible enough to accommodate the needs of the individual learner
- inform students beforehand how, when, and for what purposes they will be evaluated
- monitor program effectiveness

Although these basic principles set the general parameters for evaluation, a different approach may be more practical and useful when evaluating your evaluation on a daily basis. Any time you devise an evaluation activity, reflect on one simple question: Am I really evaluating what I think I'm evaluating?

Evaluation Pitfalls

Complex factors and unintended ambiguities can cloud and obscure what seems to be a clear and obvious task. You may intend to evaluate a specific item of learning, but wind up evaluating something totally different. Although no one who sets an evaluation activity can completely avoid the following pitfalls, everyone should keep them in mind when assessing the results.

Does the student have a reading problem?

Always assume that some students will have trouble comprehending written material.

Every class contains a range of reading levels. If the evaluative activity contains written instructions or questions, text passages, or special terminology, a student with a competent understanding of the concepts being tested but difficulties with reading may be unfairly penalized. On standardized intelligence tests, for example, good readers show up as more intelligent than poor readers. This problem also arises frequently with mathematical word problems, when students can handle the mathematics, but get lost in trying to understand the language in which the problem is expressed. The use of extensive quotes in science or history/geography quizzes causes the same consternation.

Always assume that some students will have trouble comprehending written material. If you do, you'll find yourself naturally reading aloud complex passages, explaining special terminology, and volunteering to help individuals who don't understand what certain questions or problems mean. These are worthwhile practices.

Does the student have a writing problem?

Just as every class contains a range of reading levels, every class also contains a range of writing levels. Students in varying degrees have difficulty expressing their knowledge and ability to think in written form. Their written work may also contain frequent spelling, usage, and grammatical errors or immature handwriting. These flawed surface features not only make the student material onerous to read, but also obscure the valid content that may be embedded in the answers. Too often, the material is summarily dismissed.

Regardless of how poorly or incorrectly worded a written answer may be, a limit needs to be placed on the number of marks taken off for the form of the written response and full credit reserved for a student's understanding of the issue, problem, or task.

Is the student suffering from stress?

Testing is always stressful, and the more important or rigorous the test or the more constrained the circumstances, the more stress is produced. Students who lack confidence or react adversely to pressure or who are deliberate and measured in their work habits will make errors and lose marks in spite of possessing the required skill or knowledge.

Giving students as much time for an evaluation activity as the slowest student may need will allow all students to relax and display their best efforts.

Giving students as much time for an evaluation activity as the slowest student may need will allow all students to relax and display their best efforts. Reminding students to begin with the part of the evaluation activity they find easiest lets them build confidence as they progress into the more difficult items. Offering suggestions for the maximum time that should be spent on any one aspect or item of the activity prevents students from developing tunnel vision and stalling when difficulties arise. Finally, teachers can volunteer a brief word of encouragement or guidance to students who display tension in their body language, seem bewildered or discouraged, or who are fretting over one aspect of the evaluation activity.

Is the problem the test itself?

Teachers may unwittingly devise evaluation activities with barriers that prevent some students from displaying their true capabilities. These activities should be evaluated for the following flaws:

- *Confusing terminology or instructions:* While the teacher may understand what the instruction "discuss" means, for example, students may have widely different interpretations. "Discuss" might prompt some students to tell everything they know about whatever is being asked; others might express both sides of the issue and then give their preference; and others still might analyze the issue from several different perspectives. All terminology needs to be clarified in language everyone understands. (Please see page 56 for a teacher reference sheet that gathers together a number of terms commonly used in tests, exams, and assignments, suggests a brief definition for each, and provides an example of how each might be used.)
- *Cultural skewing:* Lack of experience in the culture and norms of a test is often interpreted as limited intellectual capacity. Questions that focus on "hockey," "prom dances," or "malls," for example, contain terms or

Test or Assignment Terminology

When you build a test or prepare an assignment, you often use special terms that have precise and specific meanings. Be careful to use this terminology correctly and consistently and to ensure that your students understand what these words are directing them to do.

Direction   **Definition**

* Contrast.   Highlight the differences.
   Example: Contrast how you spend your leisure time with how your parents spend their leisure time.

* Compare.   Highlight the similarities and the differences.
   Example: Compare Superman and Batman.

* Criticize.   Make judgments about the advantages/merits and the disadvantages/faults.
   Example: Criticize the uses of nuclear power.

* Define.   Give the exact meaning and the context in which it is used.
   Example: Define the term "geopolitical."

* Evaluate.   Assess strengths and weaknesses; estimate the value of.
   Example: Evaluate recycling efforts in our community.

* Explain.   Interpret, make clear, describe, account for.
   Example: Explain the phenomenon of lightning.

* Illustrate.   Make clear or explain using examples or, when specifically directed, with diagrams, drawings, or other graphic methods.
   Example: Illustrate the water cycle using a diagram.
   Example: Illustrate with two examples from the novel *The Outsiders* that money can't buy happiness.

* Interpret.   Make the meaning clear; give your thoughts about the meaning.
   Example: Interpret Voltaire's assertion that "Labor is often the father of pleasure."

* Justify.   Prove with facts and reasoning.
   Example: Justify the effectiveness of non-violent protest.

* Outline.   Give the main points; describe in general terms.
   Example: Outline the difficulties faced by early Antarctic explorers.

* Prove.   Show something to be true by providing facts or persuasive evidence or reasoning.
   Example: Prove that humans are not the only tool-using animal.

* Summarize.   State briefly the main points or important details.
   Example: Summarize the benefits of plastic.

* Trace.   Follow the course of; describe the development of.
   Example: Trace the history of manned space flight.

concepts totally unfamiliar to some students. Activities, such as oral presentations or participation in small-group discussions, may be affected by cultural inhibitions about speaking in public or even prohibitions; in some cultures, boys and girls would never be grouped together or girls might have been taught to defer to males. For a teacher, cultural diversity in a classroom necessitates some cultural research.

- *Inappropriately interpreted results:* In some cases, while the evaluation activities may emphasize factual recall or low-level thinking skills, the results are interpreted as demonstrating higher-level thinking skills. A test of how well students have memorized capital cities, for example, has little bearing on their understanding of geographical concepts, and the grades from spelling dictations certainly don't represent the level or nature of their language fluency.

- *Misused surprise tests:* Surprise tests have a useful diagnostic or information-gathering function for both student and teacher. Students find out what they do or do not know at any particular time and can determine what kind of review and study regime they need. Teachers discover how well the learning is progressing and what kind of re-teaching or test preparation may be necessary.

   Since the students haven't had the opportunity to prepare, however, the marks from surprise tests should never be used for report card purposes. Surprise tests reward the few students with excellent natural recall, unfairly penalize students who rely on meticulous preparation for their success, and offer a ready-made excuse for those who achieve a disappointing result. Besides, students view the practice as unfair. Far from motivating students to adopt a routine of daily review for which few have the time or energy to maintain, using these marks in a summative manner only fosters resentment and discouragement.

Evaluation can never be a spontaneous activity.

   As the list of common pitfalls clearly demonstrates, evaluation can never be a spontaneous activity. While experienced teachers sometimes "fly by the seat of their pants" when presenting a lesson, they can't evaluate that way. If they understand the objectives and content of a particular lesson, recognize the options for methodology and resources, and automatically adjust what they do for the characteristics and needs of a particular class, what seems like spontaneity in presentation is really intuitive and rapid pre-planning. Evaluation, on the other hand, requires all that knowledge and experience and much, much more. The levels of complexity involved in devising a valid, fair, and effective test can be confounding.

   The main obstacle in the way of teachers implementing what they know about evaluation is time. Teachers have a limited amount of time to set tests; marking alone eats up most of the time available. The need to adhere to solid evaluation theory, applied daily, but still to attend to the never-ending pressures of time creates an understandable conundrum.

   The following teacher checklists should help resolve that problem. The first checklist establishes some general ground rules for classroom evaluation and encourages teachers to reflect on the direction they need to take within a unit or in any particular term. The questions from the checklist should be answered before planning for the unit or term begins. The second is a handy, straightforward reference to help monitor the soundness of individual tests. The tests should be created in conjunction with instructional planning.

Setting Evaluation Parameters

Before you begin instructional planning for a term or a unit, create a context for your evaluation system by reflecting on the following questions. A "No" response signifies the need for an immediate decision or declaration.

	Yes	No
• Have I decided at what points to evaluate with teacher-made tests?	❏	❏
• Will my teacher-made tests include the following techniques:		
° Essay?	❏	❏
° Open-book?	❏	❏
° Short answer?	❏	❏
° Multiple choice?	❏	❏
° True/false?	❏	❏
° Sentence matching?	❏	❏
° Fill-in-the-blank?	❏	❏
° Other? _____	❏	❏
• Will I be using a variety of other testing techniques, such as		
° Observation?	❏	❏
° Interviews or conferences?	❏	❏
° Journals, reports, or work diaries?	❏	❏
° Notebooks?	❏	❏
° Oral presentations?	❏	❏
° Projects?	❏	❏
° Performance or demonstration of skills?	❏	❏
° Other? _____	❏	❏
• Does my evaluation scheme reward process as well as product?	❏	❏
• Does my evaluation scheme reward daily work?	❏	❏
• Does my evaluation scheme reward participation?	❏	❏
• Do I have a policy for students who miss tests?	❏	❏
• Do I have a policy for retesting to improve a mark?	❏	❏
• Do I have a policy for modification of testing for students with exceptionalities?	❏	❏

How Good Is My Test?

As you begin building a specific test, use this checklist to monitor the soundness of the test and the need for modifications. A "No" response highlights an area that will require attention.

	Yes	No
• Does the test measure specific course objectives?	❏	❏
• Does the type of test match the nature of the learning I want to assess?	❏	❏
• Are the students familiar with this kind of testing?	❏	❏
• Do the students understand precisely how the test will be marked?	❏	❏
• Have the students had sufficient time to prepare for this test?	❏	❏
• Are higher-level thinking skills being tested?	❏	❏
• Are the instructions and questions clear and concise?	❏	❏
• Have the students been instructed in any specialized language or vocabulary being used?	❏	❏
• Have I decided how much weight to give the scores from this test?	❏	❏
• Have I prepared a detailed marking scheme?	❏	❏
• Am I prepared to reward unexpected, awkwardly worded, but valid answers?	❏	❏
• Have I ensured that poorer readers aren't unduly handicapped by this test?	❏	❏
• Have I ensured that facility with written language isn't unduly rewarded by this test?	❏	❏
• Does the test declare the mark distribution for each question?	❏	❏

Preparing for Projects

Formal projects come in all shapes and sizes from preparing written reports to constructing working models. They could include such features as diagrams, pictures, tables, graphs, videotapes, or CDs. Projects are assigned to either individuals or small groups of students and can involve out-of-class research and development.

Since projects arise from a unique blend of process and product goals and often include a collaborative component, evaluation becomes a complex issue. Listed below are the advantages for including projects in the curriculum. As you glance at them, consider the difficulties involved in adequately monitoring and measuring each element.

Projects offer opportunities to

- apply and practise cooperative learning skills
- learn and express learning through a variety of media and skills
- deepen learning with higher-level thinking skills
- integrate learning across the curriculum
- learn through experimentation, representation, or presentation
- reflect on and enrich learning
- individualize learning and learning strategies
- stimulate and enable the learning of others

Once a project leaves a classroom, . . . control over who did what disappears.

Each of these elements offers unique challenges for fair and equitable evaluation. Once a project leaves the classroom, for example, control over who did what disappears. Whether a project is student-completed or the product of parental or older sibling intervention is difficult to determine.

Collaboration is also a complicated and sophisticated process. Without extensive training and careful supervision, groups can encounter debilitating internal conflict and critical procedural problems. Groups may suffer personality conflicts, individuals who shirk their responsibilities, or divided perspectives on how best to proceed or divide the workload. Responsibility for completing a project can fall unfairly on one or two group members. If all members of a group receive the same mark, some members benefit from the efforts of others while some suffer for the failure of others.

As well as collaboration, projects demand a lot from students in such areas as planning, organizing, setting and adhering to timelines, revision, and self-evaluation. In a blend of process and product, however, the product and the mark it receives can easily become the overriding objective. Unless the evaluation system rewards process skills, learning will be sacrificed for product marks.

Although projects hold the potential for enabling the learning of others, the opposite is also true. When the finished projects are displayed, public comparisons of the results are inevitable, particularly if the evaluation appears on the project. For some students, self-esteem will suffer and so will their future efforts and learning.

With so many potential problems, projects are labor intensive for teachers. They have to front-load the teaching of essential skills and concepts, prepare resources and assignment instructions, and create detailed marking rubrics and instruments for monitoring groups. As work on the projects unfolds, teachers supervise their students' progress, mentoring the groups, and teaching mini-lessons. When the projects are handed in, the marking awaits.

Assigning and Marking Projects

Everything that students need or need to know about a project should be prepared in advance and presented as a package when the project is introduced. A written student outline should include the objectives of the assignment, detailed instructions for choosing and completing a topic, the due date, and a list of references and resources, if applicable.

A full and detailed evaluation rubric should be presented to the students at the same time as the assignment instructions. The rubric should contain specific evaluation criteria and the marks assigned to each element. The assignment instructions and the evaluation rubric effectively complement and reinforce each other. Marks and teacher comments should later appear only on the evaluation rubric, thereby leaving the project in pristine condition for display. This practice is a way of treating the project with respect.

To aid students in completing their projects, the work schedule should be broken up into a series of checkpoints. As groups reach each designated stage, they should confer with the teacher before moving on. At the same time, the teacher should check a group's rough work and progress reports, intervening if necessary or approving the group's decisions and progress. The teacher should also monitor adherence to timelines and the input of each group member.

If students have no control over group composition, assigning them a group mark becomes even more problematic and possibly unfair.

Some teachers encourage students to choose their own group partners while others prefer to make that decision themselves. When students are forced to work together, however, productivity and quality may suffer. As well, if students have no control over group composition, assigning them a group mark becomes even more problematic and possibly unfair. The teacher will need to ensure that individual contributions carry significant weight in the overall assessment of the group's efforts.

As much of the work as possible should be completed in the classroom or school. Each project period offers countless "teachable moments," as well as the opportunity to observe and assess interactive and process skills. Using class time for projects significantly changes students' perceptions of the activity. Rather than viewing the project as an add-on to the program or as a way to generate marks, students come to realize that the project is integral to the learning process. With project work contained in the school environment, students can still confer with friends and relatives and benefit from their advice and experience, but the task of implementing those suggestions is theirs alone.

A model project

An example of how a project might be packaged follows on pages 62 to 64. The classroom-tested project was planned as a culminating activity for a media literacy unit on stereotyping in advertising. The instruction sheet, the checkpoints sheet, and the ad evaluation sheet were presented to the intermediate students at the same time as the project was introduced. Notice that, in the case of freely chosen partnerships, specific areas of responsibility in both the planning and implementation stages had to be declared. In this way, the general mark for the project could be tempered with recognition of individual contributions.

Media Literacy Project Assignment

Topic: Image of men and women in advertising

Objectives: To review and apply the concepts and techniques of stereotyping in advertising

Assignment: Create a magazine ad that depicts several sexist and stereotypical features that make up the negative image of women and men in advertising as discussed in class. You may work by yourself or with a partner. If you decide to work with a partner, please complete the additional checkpoint information as it comes up. (Please see **Checkpoints** at the end of this assignment sheet.)

Requirements: Choose a type of product or service to advertise and identify the target audience.

- Select a name for your product or service that might appeal to your target audience and identify the kind of magazine that audience would be inclined to read. Construct a magazine ad that would appeal to your chosen readers.
- As you construct your ad, attempt to exploit the stereotypical images of women and men. Attend as well to other advertising techniques, such as type of packaging, logo, slogan, color scheme, layout, claims, and other types of written persuasion.
- Include on the back of your ad a description of and rationale for all the conscious choices you've made and the techniques you've used.
- Prepare the final ad in color on unlined paper. Size is negotiable. Since this assignment is not a test of your artistic abilities, you may include some cut-outs of people from magazines or use a guest artist for some of the drawing. Actual ads may not be used, and contributions of guest artists must be credited.

Process: Four class periods will be set aside for this assignment. All work will be done in class. A suggested timetable follows:
1. Within two periods, create a rough ad, including written description.
2. Spend two periods completing the final version.
3. Complete your sections of the ad evaluation sheet.
4. Hand in a package for marking with the final ad on top, the rough ad underneath the final ad, and the evaluation sheet on the bottom, all stapled or clipped together.

Checkpoints: A. Period one

Before moving on to your rough plan, please provide the information requested directly below, and have it checked by the teacher.

Name: _____

Name of partner (if applicable): _____

Product or service: _____

Audience for product or service: _____

Teacher signature (if approved): _____

B. Period two or three

Your rough ad and description must be approved before you move on to your final draft.

Rough ad discussed and approved unconditionally	☐
Rough ad discussed and approved with suggested changes	☐
Rough ad to be revised before approval	☐
Description discussed and approved unconditionally	☐
Description discussed and approved with suggested changes	☐
Description to be revised before approval	☐

Collaboration:

Complete this section only if you have a partner or if you plan to have a guest artist assisting you. Please indicate on the back of the sheet who has done what so far and how the rest of the work will be divided.

Explanation on back ❏   Explanation not needed ❏

Teacher signature (if approved for final draft): _____

Magazine Ad Evaluation

Student reminder: Complete self-evaluation sections, including comment, before handing in your project. Submit the final ad on top, the rough ad underneath the final ad, and the evaluation sheet on the bottom, all stapled or clipped together.

A. Please apply a letter grading (A, B, C) to each item.

    1. Rough plan complete and detailed, including description and rationale   Self ☐   Teacher ☐

    2. Written description detailed, knowledgeable, insightful   Self ☐   Teacher ☐

    3. Impact of ideas from final ad (apart from implementation)   Self ☐   Teacher ☐

    4. Implementation of ideas in final ad (carefully, attractively, inventively, skillfully completed)   Self ☐   Teacher ☐

    5. Class time used productively   Self ☐   Teacher ☐

B. Please comment on the ad features that you found most successful.

Self: _____

_____

_____

Teacher: _____

_____

_____

C. Please give the final project, including all process aspects, a letter grading.

         Self ☐   Teacher ☐

Before students began the project, they saw several videos, including Dr. Jane Kilbourne's remarkable analysis of print ads in *Still Killing Us Softly*, produced by Cambridge Documentary Films. The students were well versed in the techniques and values commonly on display in print advertising; they had analyzed and discussed hundreds of ads from a wide variety of magazines and newspapers.

As the instruction sheet reflects, students were challenged to write in role as ad designers seeking to craft highly effective and persuasive messages and images, and then reflect on how they accomplished their goals. By intellectually constructing and deconstructing their own ads, students were able to gain fresh insight into the effects of the countless images around them and to express what they learned pointedly and succinctly in the language of print ads themselves.

Completed projects should also have a purpose beyond the individual or group learning process. They can be valuable additions to stimulate and consolidate the learning of everyone in the class. Teachers can easily set up a questionnaire or observation sheet, for example, based on a display of the projects. In the media literacy project just outlined, after the evaluation sheets were removed, the projects were displayed throughout the room in groups of four or five. Students were assigned to a group of projects and directed to identify an example of a stereotyping technique from each project. The students were then reconvened in small discussion groups to share their findings.

Research and the Internet

Although not true of the sample project, research plays a major role in most classroom projects. Research inside or outside of the school automatically brings you face to face with the mixed blessings of the Internet.

In this computer age, teachers are too apt to credit students with a greater degree of computer literacy than they possess. Travel on the information highway is a case in point. For many students, research and the Internet have become almost synonymous; the Internet is often their first and only port of call when a project is assigned. Point, click, copy, and the research is done — the Internet as infallible oracle has all the answers.

Students need help if they're going to use the Internet successfully.

Students need help if they're going to use the Internet successfully. They need to appreciate both the strengths and the weaknesses of the Internet to free themselves from an unquestioning dependence on a relatively limited and unreliable source of information. They need to understand that the use of the Internet in school research projects is problematic for three main reasons:

1. It's one tool, not the only tool.
   Many students work under the assumption that only the Internet has what they need. They feel they have to use the computer; if they can't use the computer, they can't do research.
2. The Internet doesn't have a brain.
   Many students think that the Internet knows more than they do. In their minds, a typographical error in their search request makes no difference — the Internet can figure out what they want; a negative search means no information exists.

3. The effective use of the Internet requires the application of a highly sophisticated set of interrelated skills that students may not have.
   • Many students lack criteria for selecting the appropriate search engine.
   • A simple search often produces a list of hundreds of sites. Students are presented with too many choices and too much information.
   • Many students have difficulty with the concept of a search. They expect the Internet to operate much like an encyclopedia: simply type in your topic and the answer will pop up. They have difficulty narrowing their searches.
   • Few students possess the criteria for deciding on the usefulness of one site over another.
   • Few students possess the background information to evaluate the authenticity and validity of a site.
   • The material is often at an adult reading level.
   • "Point and click" impulses take over from reading and discriminating among the images on the screen. Students seldom read instructions.
   • Non-thinking activities, such as copying and printing pictures and graphics, are a priority.
   • Plagiarism is a constant concern. Students download and print material without change or even without comprehension and claim it as their own.
   • Many students have difficulty staying on task: too many distractions unrelated to their search are a "click" away.

Often neglected and underused, on-line encyclopedia and CD-ROMs offer a viable alternative to the Internet. The material in these forms is organized and categorized; information is easy to find, up-to-date, authentic, and valid. The articles are concise, easy to skim and scan, and written at a reading level that's appropriate for full comprehension.

Like the Internet, on-line encyclopedia and CD-ROMs possess disadvantages. Articles are often too brief for comprehensive, in-depth treatments, and material does not cover up-to-the-moment current events unless augmented by special electronic newspaper and periodical library programs.

Regardless of the advantages of on-line encyclopedia and CD-ROMs and the difficulties involved in using the Internet for research, students will be drawn inexorably to the Internet. Since forewarned is forearmed, the guideline on page 67 offers them a variety of tips to help make their passage through the Internet maze more efficient and effective.

How to Use the Internet

- Qualify your search as specifically and narrowly as you can, for example, not "Civil War" but "Civil War Union uniforms."

- Reject any sites that offer a chance to win a prize or that advertise a service or product.

- Skim the first paragraph; if the material is difficult to understand, leave the site.

- Skim the length of the material; if there's a lot of material and no table of contents or index, leave the site, or be prepared to invest a lot of time with no guarantee of success.

- Check the authenticity of the site with the teacher or librarian; better yet, ask the teacher to bookmark recommended sites for quick access.

- Stay on task; avoid distractions. If you accidentally log on to an inappropriate site, log off immediately.

- If you haven't answered your question or found some relevant material on a site after about five minutes, consider moving on to another site.

Essay-style Evaluation

Writing essays is hard; writing essays without the proper opportunity to reflect and revise is hard indeed.

Writing essays is hard; writing essays without the proper opportunity to reflect and revise is hard indeed. When teachers attempt to assess higher-level thinking skills, however, they often turn to the essay. Ideally, an essay allows students to explore concepts in depth, to organize and synthesize information, and to present their arguments in a coherent, logical, and persuasive manner. An essay-style test is well suited to making comparisons, especially among disparate elements, formulating and proving hypotheses, or detailing and explaining complex ideas or processes.

The downside, of course, is that relatively few students have writing skills sophisticated enough to move their essays much beyond a recitation of memorized facts. An essay answer often becomes a kind of all-purpose container into which students pour whatever they know about a particular topic. These students usually lack the writing skills necessary to present that content clearly and coherently. In these cases, the form of the questioning actually blocks the function; the testing format interferes with the testing process.

Essay writing depends on revision: a recurrent process of rethinking and rewriting. Except for a fortunate few, the time limits of a test or exam situation truncate this process and can even produce additional stress that further interferes with cognitive function. Rather than another kind of learning experience, the essay can quickly turn into a minefield of frustrations.

Students need as much practice as possible writing expository essays. The logical and sequential format of an essay should be a familiar and comfortable structure: they outline precisely what they are planning to investigate or prove, set up a series of proofs or arguments to persuade the reader, and conclude by restating whatever they've proven in a dramatic, emphatic, or memorable way. Of course, the age and abilities of any particular class should determine how often this type of questioning is used in a test or exam and how much weight the marks carry in any overall assessment of progress.

As well as learning how to write essays, students of all ages can also benefit from direct instruction in how to write an essay-style test or exam. The next student guideline serves as a practical, step-by-step checklist to help students prepare for and master the intricacies of answering essay-style questions.

How to Write an Essay-style Test

Please place a check mark beside each of the following steps and actions you normally take when writing a test. Put a question mark beside the ones you normally skip over or don't use. When you get to the end of the questionnaire, consider the items with question marks and circle those you intend to begin using.

When answering an essay-style test or exam, do you

- begin by reading all instructions and questions? (Notice how many of the succeeding actions depend on this first step.) ❑

- underline or circle key words or phrases in the questions, such as "compare," "list four causes," or "explain with a diagram"? ❑

- note which questions are worth more than others? (A question worth twice as much as another deserves more time and consideration.) ❑

- figure out how much time to spend on each question and stick to that timetable? (Trying to say too much can be as inefficient as waiting for inspiration.) ❑

- start with the question that you know most about — not necessarily the first question on the paper? (If you keep each extended answer on separate sheets of paper, you can always reorder them at the end if that's a priority for your teacher.) ❑

- leave the questions about which you are most uncertain until near the end of your allotted time? (Spend your time on what you know; what you don't know won't get you any more marks.) ❑

- skip a question if you don't know the answer? (After you answer what you know, you can go back to these problematic questions; if you sit for too long over an answer you don't know, you leave little time for the answers you do know.) ❑

- before answering a question, list in point form on a separate sheet of paper the key ideas or points that come immediately to mind? (You'll relieve the stress of trying to remember every detail, and you'll be able to organize and shape your answer.) ❑

- match what you know to what is being asked? ❑

  Example: If the question asks for a specific number of causes, choose from your list the most important.

  Example: If the question is worth six marks and asks for two causes, you know you'll need to elaborate or expand on those two causes.

- determine how many paragraphs will suit your answer? ❑

  (Make it as easy as possible for a reader to understand what you're saying. One important concept with supporting details per paragraph is a good rough guide.)

- write on every other line? (Doing so will allow you to make later ❑
  corrections or additions more easily, and the answer will be easier to read.)

- include the key words or phrases from the question in the introductory ❑
  portion of your answer? (You and your reader will stay focused on the requirements of the question.)

- state your position or opinion, if requested, and shape your answer to ❑
  support and validate that stand?

- conclude your answer by indicating clearly what you've shown or proved? ❑

- leave a space of at least a few lines at the end of each answer in case you ❑
  think of a point to add before you have to hand in your paper?

Objective-style Evaluation

Objective-style test items, such as multiple choice, true/false, or fill-in-the-blank, have one major attraction for teachers: they're all easier and faster to mark than essay-style questions. They also offer students certain general advantages over essay-style questions: writing proficiency has no bearing on the results, marking is more objective, and the results will pinpoint precisely what students do and do not know.

Objective-style test items also possess distinct disadvantages when compared with essay-style testing:

- They often emphasize only factual recall, a low-level thinking skill.
- Although writing proficiency is not a factor in the testing, reading proficiency can skew the results.
- Although marking time for teachers is greatly reduced, preparation of good objective-style questions consumes time.
- The responses leave no trace of a student's thinking processes.

The different types of objective-style questions echo these general advantages and disadvantages to varying degrees. In multiple choice testing, for instance, a question is followed by a number of responses at least one of which is correct. This technique requires no writing skills, offers prompts to cue memory, can be easily and quickly marked and analyzed, and lends itself to computerized testing. On the other hand, the following sample test item highlights several additional disadvantages:

Why should teachers be cautious when contemplating a multiple choice test?
a. The questions could actually be a test of reading proficiency.
b. Good questions are difficult and time consuming to construct.
c. This type of question seldom tests higher-level thinking skills.
d. All of the above.

With multiple choice, process of elimination also augments the potential for guessing. In the example above, if you know that at least two of the responses are correct, then "d. All of the above" has to be correct. Unless the test items are constructed carefully and designed for a specific group of students, the disadvantages can easily overcome the test's usefulness.

True/false testing is popular for many of the same reasons as multiple choice: no writing skills are required, it lends itself to computerization, and it's quickly and easily marked. In true/false testing, students must decide whether or not a statement is correct. Although widely used, the format has some built-in problems.

Mainly superficial or trivial items lend themselves readily to true/false testing.

True/false testing, which almost exclusively tests factual recall, encourages guessing. Some teachers, of course, discourage guessing by subtracting incorrect answers from the total correct. That practice discourages any kind of risk taking and leaves the teacher in the unenviable position of justifying why a correct answer is neutralized and discredited by a totally unrelated question. In this situation, marks, not learning, become the focus. Besides, depending on students' personalities, subtracting "wrongs" from "rights" can have two opposite effects. Some students will continue to guess and will consequently do better than chance; others will be afraid to mark anything but answers of which they are totally sure, thereby omitting many items they otherwise would have had a good chance of answering correctly.

True/false questioning has another significant disadvantage that arises with items such as the following:

A standardized reading test is a valid measure of an individual's reading abilities. True or false?

In this case, the more you know about reading and standardized testing, the more you second-guess yourself as you try to answer the question. If you answer the question from the point of view of an administrator who's introduced and implemented standardized reading tests, the answer could be true. If you answer from the point of view of a reading specialist, you'd say false. If you're a professional evaluator, however, you'd want to answer "maybe."

Mainly superficial or trivial items lend themselves readily to true/false testing. Across the curriculum, significant chunks of the curriculum just can't be categorized in absolute terms. As a consequence, teachers are forced into removing statements from texts and converting them into incorrect statements. Too often, the statements are either obviously wrong or so ambiguous that only the most proficient readers spot the discrepancies from the original statements.

These problems also plague short answer questions, such as fill-in-the-blanks or sentence completion, as the next example illustrates:

Objective-style questions are easy to _____.

If teachers answered the question, the word "mark" would probably first spring to mind to complete the sentence. On reflection, they might also respond with "write," or "criticize," or "computerize." With so many possible answers, the item is fatally flawed. The more that a marker needs to evaluate answers to objective-style questions, the more the key advantage to using this type of testing disappears. Narrowing the choices to only one is also problematic. The more time spent on creating effective, valid, and thought-provoking questions, the less objective-style testing appeals to time-strapped teachers.

Deus ex Machina: The Computer

Computer technology is insidiously beguiling.

We teach; we test. When we test, we're turning more and more to objective-style testing. With all the complications and problems associated with this type of testing, why is the use of objective-style testing so widespread and so prevalent? The answer, of course, is computers.

When ancient Greek playwrights had insoluble plotlines remaining at the end of a play, they often dangled a deity on the end of a hoist, called a "machina," over the stage and lowered the god to the ground to resolve all matters in an all-knowing, all-powerful manner. Computers seem to be our version of the *deus ex machina.*

Computer technology is insidiously beguiling. As a matter of course, vast quantities of data are instantly tabulated and manipulated, personal communication is opened to every corner of the world, and countless, tedious tasks are transformed and facilitated. Unlike the anthropomorphic Greek gods, moreover, computers are endorsed as neutral tools, by definition disinterested and objective. On the other hand, to be truly efficient, computers need to interface with reality in a distinct and demanding manner. Therein lies the rub.

Human experience must first be objectively defined in terms of observable or quantifiable behavior before it can be analyzed via computer. The form into which experience must be rendered determines whether or not the computer can perform its assessment functions. In education, function should always determine form; the needs of the individual learner determine how the curriculum is delivered. In the world of computers, the opposite is often true. The nature or form of the Internet, for example, will determine its ultimate use.

In computer-assisted research, certain types of questions are more cost-effective than others. In education, skill and drill and graphics programs, information transmission, and word processing have most easily emerged from the computer's capabilities.

In computer-assisted assessment, factual recall is the most easily tested aspect of learning. Personal reflection is the most difficult to test, as well as the most expensive. Which will be most often used?

The danger, of course, is that learning may increasingly be subsumed by education's investment in computers. What the computer does well, will increase; whatever fits awkwardly or not at all into that science will fall away.

At the same time, the nature of computers has affected how curriculum is structured, assessed, and even thought about. Curriculum is being translated into discrete items, logically arranged in scope and sequence, interwoven with regular, periodic feedback assessment, and supported by similarly structured support materials. In effect, mastery learning has mutated into computer-assisted education.

The nature of computers has led programmers to seamlessly integrate individualized teaching and testing in their programs in a way few flesh-and-blood teachers ever could. In this computerized teaching model, a pretest first determines an area of weakness or a level of expertise. Based on that information, the student is led through a teaching experience followed by a practice session. A posttest determines the student's success rate and directs the student either into a remedial exercise or on to the next area of weakness or up to the next level. The program also presents the teacher with a profile of the student's strengths and weaknesses, a record of the student's progress, a score derived from the student's activities, and homework questions based on the profile. The process is interactive, efficient, and independent of the teacher.

The theory may appear sound, but the application of this kind of computerized, behaviorist teaching and testing is both limited and limiting. First and foremost, computers are best suited to rote learning and objective-style evaluation; the more you incorporate computers in a mastery learning model for your subject area, the more you are focusing on and rewarding factual recall and lower-level thinking skills. If your evaluation is narrow and mechanical, then that is what your curriculum will be.

Since computers operate in a linear, step-by-step manner, computer programs assume that learning also operates in a rigidly controlled, regulated, and carefully managed manner. Much learning, on the other hand, appears from outside the learner to be haphazard, unpredictably recursive and individualistic, egocentric, and just plain messy. Computer programs can't accommodate this learning model.

Computerized learning/teaching programs make a number of options available to each student, but the process is far from individualized. Factors such as learning style, motivation, reading proficiency, background experiences, and learning exceptionalities are seldom accommodated in the learning experiences or incorporated into the computer's evaluation system.

How and how often these kinds of computer programs are used to further curriculum goals and meet student needs, of course, rest on the judgment and intervention of teachers. Unfortunately, teachers in many educational systems are feeling the pressures of computer-driven learning/teaching environments.

Once a school or board of education invests heavily in computer technology, the need for accountability begins to drive the program: the more the computers are used, the more justified the expense.

When the need for accountability expands into the curriculum itself, moreover, computers are the medium and the message. If a curriculum is articulated in a series of discrete, computer-friendly statements, computerized report cards are a few keystrokes away; if the series of discrete, computer-friendly curriculum statements are incorporated into the teach-test framework of computerized educational programs, then the circle is complete. Classroom teaching and learning, individual student assessment, reporting to parents, and system accountability are instantly harmonized.

Most educational systems have also developed detailed, multi-year plans for large-scale assessments of student achievement. These schemes usually include the provision that the results be interpreted and reported publicly for the use of educators and the community at large. Assessment on this massive a scale, keyed to and integrated with specific curricular outcomes and resource materials, could be attempted only with the aid of computer technology. No wonder the pressure increases daily to make education and computer technology synonymous. As the two become welded together, a crucial question emerges: Are we redefining education to better fit the limitations of computers, or redefining the role of computers to better fill the needs of education?

Educational institutions are slow to adapt to change, though. In the case of schools adapting to and integrating computer technology, that flaw may be a hidden strength. Until computer technology can begin to accommodate the depth, complexities, and individual needs of learners, teachers will have to continue finding ways to keep the curriculum from shrinking to the boundaries of computerized evaluation. As Albert Einstein observed, "Not everything that can be counted, counts. Not everything that counts, can be counted."

It's up to classroom teachers to continue to create evaluation systems that emphasize formative growth and that reward individual progress and higher-level thinking. Computer technology is firmly entrenched in the educational environment and, for good and bad, will increasingly influence what goes on in classrooms. If evaluation is the head of the educational horse, computer technology now serves as the reins. Reins are sometimes needed for control and direction, but can't supplant the intelligence and power of the horse itself.

Are we redefining education to better fit the limitations of computers, or redefining the role of computers to better fill the needs of education?

The Learning and Language Dilemma

"I teach and they're supposed to learn,
but so many students at this level still have problems
reading, writing, or even speaking that their learning is affected.
The classes are large and the curriculum is challenging:
what can I do to help them?"

Nothing about teaching is ever simple and straightforward, especially not the relationship between learning and language.

The way our schools are organized, for example, would make you believe that learning and language are separate and distinct processes. Our curriculum guides, daily timetables, and report cards separate learning into subject areas, one of which is language arts or English. We're assigned areas of responsibility based on these divisions. When it's time for Math, we teach math; when it's time for Science, we teach science; and we expect the language arts or English teacher to accept responsibility for teaching reading, writing, listening, and speaking. Schools may be organized that way, but as any teacher soon discovers, learning isn't.

You Say Learning; I Say Language

For all practical purposes, learning and language are intrinsically linked.

The work of learning in schools is not just language based, but literacy based. The more proficient the student is at reading and writing, the more able the student is to handle school tasks across the curriculum. For all practical purposes, learning and language are intrinsically linked.

Learning may, at any one time, incorporate some or all aspects of language. By the same token, the act of processing language involves more than communicating or recording experience. Through language, people construct their sense of reality by revealing, clarifying, discovering, assessing, reflecting on, and refining what they think and feel about experience.

Language development is a natural and purposeful process occurring in different ways and at different times and rates for each individual. The individualized and personal nature of language development has an essential and far-reaching impact on how teachers structure learning. Language facility is one of the most important variables affecting how an individual processes experience. At all times, teachers have to defer to a student's need to make sense of the world through language and attempt to instruct in the context of that student's own language practice.

Teachers have to appreciate a student's intelligence and understanding apart from that student's facility with reading, writing, listening, and speaking. When students experience difficulty in any subject area, they have to decide how much of that problem can be attributed to language and how much to learning. When they structure a learning experience for students, they always have to accommodate the range in their language fluency. Nothing in teaching is harder to do.

Reading to Learn

Children come to school at varying stages of reading development; some already read confidently and independently, and some won't reach that stage for two or three years. Even as children enter Kindergarten, a gap is already apparent between those who have an obvious facility with reading and those who are diagnosed "at risk" of developing reading difficulties. As children move through their school years, that gap grows larger, with students at all levels ranging along a spectrum of varying attitudes toward and facility with reading.

Regardless of grade level, teachers can never assume that all students possess the requisite reading skills. All teachers, especially at the intermediate and secondary school levels, have to acknowledge and attend to that range. Reading and learning are not synonymous, but as students move through the grades, reading fluency and success in school become interconnected: there is an increasing reliance on a text-driven curriculum.

The Trouble with Texts

Most textbooks are a barrier to learning for all of the students some of the time and some of the students all of the time.

As students advance through the grades, they face an ever-increasing array of textbooks. Texts encapsulate what parents, politicians, and many teachers expect from schools. The learning is prescribed in scope and sequence, standardized, teacher directed, and easily described, managed, and evaluated. Unfortunately, most textbooks are a barrier to learning for all of the students some of the time and some of the students all of the time. The source of the difficulties that students encounter when trying to learn from textbooks is threefold: what students bring to the texts, how teachers use the texts, and the nature of the texts themselves.

Any classroom at any grade level contains a range of reading proficiencies. From the early primary grades, the gap between most and least proficient grows wider year after year. Every time a teacher prescribes a text-based assignment, the results are handicapped: the better readers will understand the content better than the poorer readers. The range in reading proficiency will also be reflected in the range of difficulty that students encounter with a text. Some students comprehend perfectly, some not at all, and most fall somewhere inbetween. Unless teachers implement strategies to help students unlock meaning from texts, dependent readers are constantly in a state of double jeopardy: not only do they struggle in their English/language arts classes, their difficulties with reading also undermine their efforts to learn in every subject across the curriculum.

Students need daily support in how to manage the content in textbooks, but rarely receive it. Research has demonstrated that teachers seldom see themselves in that support role and, if they do, seem uncertain about how to help. Teachers still devote much of their time, for example, to assigning and marking work and relatively little time to explaining and modelling thinking processes. The most used reading activities involve recalling, copying, and demonstrating facts: in other words, asking students to prove that they read what they were supposed to read. The least used reading activities involve summarizing or synthesizing. Students are seldom asked to reflect thoughtfully on the material they read.

Students are seldom asked to reflect thoughtfully on the material they read.

More often than not, teachers designate a certain number of pages in a text, assign questions based on that material, and expect written answers from their students. They assume that asking the questions will stimulate reflection and that answering the questions will forge understanding. Their faith in this process is misguided. As Richard Allington, a noted authority on literacy, says, "Asking questions does little to foster thinking and question answering provides little good evidence of understanding." Students require more than questions to help them sort out the meaning locked in texts.

Deciphering Textbooks

Textbooks are often hard to read. They are unable to serve the multiple reading levels and vast range of interests and backgrounds found in an average class. When subject to a jargon-filled academic style, they are likely full of endless detail, tortuous, technical explanations, and few metaphors. Textbook authors are experts in their fields and their field is rarely reading comprehension. Their books are usually high on concept load and elevated in reading level. While the style creates a barrier for all but the better readers, the dense content itself gives rise to another problem affecting everyone. Without a lot of background in a particular area, students encounter even more difficulty making sense of the material in the text.

The words on a page become meaningful only when infused with experience, real or vicarious. A manual on operating a word-processing program is impenetrable if you've never sat in front of a computer screen, but explodes with meaning when you're ready to compose on your first PC. In the same way, a picture can instantly illuminate a thousand words written about the Rocky Mountains. Comprehension is directly affected by an individual's experiences and the beliefs and values developed from those experiences. In short, the more you know about a specific topic before you begin reading, the more you understand from the reading; conversely, the less you know beforehand, the less you comprehend from the text.

In any text-based assignment, students need strategies to help them comprehend the material and, in the process, build bridges between their own experiences and the new experiences embedded in the text. Teachers can help by using some of the following strategies when designing lessons based on a text:

- Read aloud sample passages from the text and model the thought processes involved in making sense of the material. (What goes through your mind as

Encourage the use of response journals, in which students can reflect on the content in a personally significant manner, make comparisons and inferences, and expand on the text.

you read? What connections are you making to your own life and experiences? What questions are springing to your mind?)
- Read aloud supplementary and illuminating reference material, such as eyewitness accounts, vivid descriptions, unusual perspectives or opinions.
- Provide students with similar supplementary material with a range of reading levels.
- Supply a context in which to set the reading through such devices and activities as pictures, videos, diagrams, anecdotes, or hands-on experiences.
- Create time in class for students to actively read the text.
- Encourage students to ask questions about their reading without fear of embarrassment or of being judged inadequate.
- Organize opportunities for students to discuss the reading in pairs or in small groups. (The more they share insights, difficulties, questions, concerns, and strategies, the more clues they gather in their struggle to figure the text out.)
- Encourage students to relate and integrate what they're reading to their own experiences or vicarious experiences from books and media.
- Offer students a variety of strategies to comprehend material, such as these:
  - hypothesizing, including predicting outcomes or asking "what if . . . ?"
  - formulating their own questions
  - distinguishing cause-and-effect relationships
  - defining problems
  - distinguishing fact from opinion
  - selecting criteria to make assessments
  - justifying points of view
  - recognizing central meanings and generalizing
  - drawing conclusions
  - making inferences and judgments
  - dramatizing
  - representing through other media
- Decide what activities would function more effectively before or during rather than after the actual reading.
- Encourage the use of response journals, in which students can reflect on the content in a personally significant manner, make comparisons and inferences, and expand on the text.

This last strategy is especially important. Given the diversity of our school populations and the individual differences of background, ability, experiences, and culture, response journals are an essential tool. They also exemplify how the concept of learning through language needs to be applied across the curriculum.

Writing to Learn

Every student in every classroom knows the routine: write, revise, edit, hand in for marking. Whether it's an essay for History, a project in Science, or a research assignment in Mathematics, the drill's the same. With word processing tailor-made for the writing process, even homework assignments based on textbooks go through the same cycle.

This emphasis on a process orientation has obscured the many other valid and vital reasons for writing. Writing to record ideas, facts, or experiences for oneself, as well as for others, for example, is an essential life skill. Even more important is the realization that writing and thinking are so closely linked that, for many people, they're interdependent. In this case, thinking through a problem or issue for oneself rather than communicating with others becomes the goal; reflection is the process and writing is the key.

When students try to learn through writing, the rules about what their writing might look like or how it might be treated have to change.

When students try to learn through writing, the rules about what their writing might look like or how it might be treated have to change. Across the curriculum, when students learn through language, that use of language can be hesitant, tentative, halting, repetitive, and recursive. When they learn through writing, the process is "messy." The goal is understanding. As understanding is achieved and the goal becomes communication, fluency improves. But if students focus on fluency before achieving the goal of communication, understanding is impaired.

Our decades-long emphasis on a writing process, however, has students monitoring every word they write for errors. They do this before they've even thought through what they're trying to say. As a result, an uncomfortable language dichotomy has emerged: personal, informal language is permitted in discussion situations and discouraged in most kinds of written work.

This confusion between ends and means in writing is readily apparent even when reflective, written language is the goal. The widespread use of learning logs and response journals of all kinds acknowledges how essential a student's personal language is in learning. This approach directs students to examine the crucial link between how they learn and what they learn. The common practice of marking surface errors or mode of expression in logs and journals, though, undermines their purpose.

In any effective writing program, ends and means must be complementary. The steps in a writing process, for example, become mindless drill when the writer has nothing to say. By the same token, if the goal is to reflect on or extend learning, that process necessarily becomes an end in itself. In either case, the imposition of the revising/editing cycle would be counterproductive.

The critical role that writing plays in thinking and learning can be reaffirmed without disrupting the benefits derived from the writing process movement. If the function of the writing determines the nature of the process, a balance among writing's various roles across the curriculum can be achieved.

Duelling Journals

The proliferation of journal writing in all subject areas has led to much confusion about what journals are, how and when they should be used, and how to evaluate them. Learning logs, work diaries, subject-specific journals, and response journals all refer to informal writing to facilitate learning. Since they differ significantly from one another, though, you may find the following descriptions helpful.

- *Learning logs/Work diaries:* day-to-day written records of what is done in a particular subject area and what and how students are learning; they are commonly used when students are working independently for extended periods, such as on projects.
- *Subject-specific journals:* similar to a log or work diary, but including information on how students feel about what they're doing, as well as a formative

self-evaluation component; these grew out of the recognition of the importance of metacognition in learning, but without the reliance on personal response (explanations of metacognition and personal response follow these descriptions); these journals can be applied to any unit of study in any subject area.

- *Response journal:* a notebook, folder, section of a binder, or electronic file in which students record their personal reactions to, questions about, and reflections on what they read, view, write, represent, observe, listen to, discuss, do, and think and how they go about reading, viewing, writing, representing, observing, listening, discussing, or doing; first used extensively in English/language arts programs; it can be adapted to any unit of study in any subject area.

Metacognition, noted as a factor in subject-specific journals, refers to the ability to reflect on and talk about thinking; specifically, learners begin to focus on their patterns of thought and become aware of how and, eventually, why they process experience the way they do. This ability is enhanced by developmental factors and encouraged by reflective educational practices.

The concept of personal response, although not relevant to subject-specific journals, lies at the heart of response journals. In reading, for example, readers are asked to make connections and build bridges between their own reading and the previous vicarious and real experiences that might have influenced their interpretation of what they've read. Response journals recognize that comprehension springs from the mind, not the page.

Through personal response, learning is personalized, deepened, and extended, and higher-level thinking processes are regularly addressed. Indeed, personal response is ideally suited to the vagaries and messiness of many higher-level thinking skills. It captures everything from the unpredictability of the individual paths leading to insight to the emotional, subjective content of understanding and memory.

This kind of writing-to-learn is tricky to implement, mainly because a process approach to writing is so firmly entrenched in many teachers' minds. One prevalent misconception about journal writing, for example, either undermines the effectiveness of the approach or prevents teachers from using it. Teachers are quick to declare that they don't have the time to read and mark these journals every day — they don't realize that they shouldn't be marking surface features at all.

Teachers tend to respond reflexively to the spelling mistakes and grammatical errors they find in journals. Since for so long they've heard the cry that "every teacher is an English teacher," they assume that they're compelled to identify and have their students correct all the surface errors that students make in their informal writing. Nothing could be further from the truth.

A student's personal language is essential to the learning process. Informal, natural, and spontaneous, it reflects how the mind deals with assorted facts, impressions, memories, and feelings. When students write in their journals in this mode, surface errors are common, but these do not impede the learning process and learning is, after all, the primary goal. If the goal were communication with others, then students would have to take a more rigorous approach to the writing process. They would draft, revise, edit, proofread, and make the writing public. But a personal response is not a formal essay.

Response journals recognize that comprehension springs from the mind, not the page.

If surface features or modes of expression in journals were marked, the outpouring of thoughts and feelings would be impeded and students would be much more reluctant to take risks. What they were attempting to understand would become secondary to whether or not a particular word was spelled correctly. The spontaneous flow of language and thought would be destroyed.

How to Mark Journals

So, how exactly should journals be evaluated? Their purpose governs the criteria. Since response journals direct students to examine the crucial link between how and what they learn, evaluation should be based on learning criteria rather than on fluency criteria. Teachers can look at journal marking in two ways: short term and long term.

In the short term — every week or so, for instance — teachers want to let students know at what level they're functioning in their journals and what they need to do to improve. They also need to keep marking fast and efficiently to stay on top of the quantity of material. Devising and posting a simple rubric divided into levels and explained with criteria and a percentage range for each level is a popular solution. The levels are linked to the performance criteria already established and introduced when journals are introduced. A check mark or color code will indicate to students how well they're progressing. The rubric contains the information necessary for students to understand what they need to do to improve.

The rubric on page 82 names the levels for clarification and includes a possible mark range. You could use a series of check marks or some other designation scheme. Avoid using letters, though. A letter designation, such as A, B, C, or D, carries many summative connotations and denotations. You want to let students know how well they're progressing without weighting each short-term segment with a summative grade.

The sample rubric arbitrarily employs four levels. Students at any one level will often display characteristics from another level. The degree to which their profiles overlap determines whether or not they would be achieving at the lower or upper end of the mark range. Teachers should match their own levels with their summative reporting standards.

When teachers need to generate a mark from a student's journal entries, perhaps at the end of a unit or before a reporting period, they can easily develop a summative evaluation instrument using the short-term criteria. (See page 83.)

A certain level of legibility and readability is necessary in notebooks, note pads, learning logs, work diaries, subject-specific journals, and response journals. Although the writing is a medium for thought and for learning, it will likely be used later. Students will use it either as first-draft material for essays, as resource material for projects, or for studying; teachers will review it to assess the learning that it represents. Since spelling mistakes, usage errors, and passable handwriting don't interfere with the purposes for such writing, though, they shouldn't play a role in the evaluation criteria. With the vise-like grip of constantly producing print-ready writing loosened, both students and teachers benefit. Students are empowered to learn through their writing, and teachers are freed from the senseless "donkey work" of editing every word their students write. Everybody wins.

The rubric contains the information necessary for students to understand what they need to do to improve.

Short-term Marking Rubric for Response Journal Entries

Level	Percentage Range	Criteria
Non-compliant	below 50%	- insufficient number and/or length of responses - responses usually perfunctory and superficial - personal connections seldom explored and analyzed - insufficient understanding of content evident
Compliant	50–65%	- sufficient number and/or length of responses - responses on-topic and thoughtful - personal connections usually explored and analyzed - satisfactory understanding of content apparent - some evidence of higher-level thinking, e.g., defining problems, linking cause and effect, selecting and applying criteria, drawing conclusions, justifying points of view, formulating own questions, generating hypotheses
Extended	66–79%	- more than sufficient number and/or length of responses - responses on-topic, thoughtful, and reflective - personal connections always explored and analyzed - superior understanding of content apparent - frequent evidence of higher-level thinking, e.g., defining problems, linking cause and effect, selecting and applying criteria, drawing conclusions, justifying points of view, formulating own questions, generating hypotheses
Independent	80% +	- considerably more than sufficient number and/or length of responses - responses on-topic, thoughtful, reflective, and insightful - personal connections always explored and analyzed in depth - mature understanding of content apparent - considerable evidence of higher-level thinking, e.g., defining problems, linking cause and effect, selecting and applying criteria, drawing conclusions, justifying points of view, formulating own questions, generating hypotheses

Teacher Guideline

Long-term Evaluation Instrument
for Response Journal Entries

To what extent do the entries indicate that the student has

	Non-compliant (0–4 marks)	Compliant (5–6 marks)	Extended (7–8 marks)	Independent (9–10 marks)
• responded in number and/or at length?	☐	☐	☐	☐
• responded on-topic, thoughtfully, and reflectively?	☐	☐	☐	☐
• explored and analyzed personal connections?	☐	☐	☐	☐
• acquired a mature understanding of the content covered?	☐	☐	☐	☐
• demonstrated evidence of higher-level thinking skills?	☐	☐	☐	☐

Examples include defining problems, linking cause and effect, selecting and applying criteria, drawing conclusions, justifying points of view, formulating own questions, and generating hypotheses.

Total: ☐ /50

Talking and Learning

Schools are talk factories.

Schools are talk factories: teachers talk, students talk, and sometimes everybody talks at the same time. In the classroom setting, directions are given, questions asked and answered, and discussions occur. Since thinking and language are, for all practical purposes, inseparable, learning happens best in a language-based, talk-driven curriculum. For students to learn through talk, however, they need to be convinced that what they are saying is more important than how they are saying it. As students examine, organize, think through, and reflect on what and how they learn, they need to speak naturally and spontaneously, as they do in everyday conversation.

Various uses of talk in the classroom vary in effectiveness. The least effective application is the lecture model, where a teacher talks and the class listens and supposedly learns. The most effective use of talk for learning occurs in small-group cooperative discussions. A quasi-Socratic form of mind-reading usually occupies the uneasy middle ground between the two: the teacher asks questions to which she or he already knows the answers and expects students to phrase the answers in a particular way.

None of this classroom talk, regardless of structure, happens automatically. Careful planning is necessary before classroom talk functions effectively. If students aren't practising and applying the necessary talk-based skills, they'll need specific direction and teaching.

A useful exercise before teaching any lesson is to target the specific skills you want your students to apply during their discussions. After the lesson, determine the skills that the students actually used. You can also look over a unit's work in the same way. This exercise is a useful reminder not to take student-talk for granted.

You can also examine the profile of talk-based skills and target specific skills that may need emphasis. The checklist on page 85 demonstrates how this analysis might be accomplished.

Small-Group Discussions

The most effective and efficient way to harness and focus student-talk for the purpose of learning is through small-group discussions. In these discussions, students interact with and learn from one another. Such cooperative learning is one of the most powerful learning/teaching strategies at a teacher's disposal. Collaborative problem-solving can be used effectively with all age groups and in any subject area.

Implementation of cooperative learning strategies has consistently yielded wide-ranging benefits:

- higher academic achievement
- improved learning results, especially for average students and students "at risk"
- more effective problem solving
- increased higher-level thinking skills
- more positive attitudes toward subject
- greater motivation to learn

Teacher Checklist

Talk-based Learning

Please complete the appropriate designation:

Lesson: _____

Unit: _____

Period of time: _____

Skill Bank	Targeted Skills (Please check prior to lesson.)	Applied Skills (Please check after lesson.)
defining problems	❏	❏
generating hypotheses	❏	❏
reasoning	❏	❏
predicting	❏	❏
selecting criteria to make assessments	❏	❏
justifying points of view	❏	❏
explaining	❏	❏
formulating questions	❏	❏
drawing conclusions	❏	❏
imagining	❏	❏
clarifying	❏	❏
observing/reporting	❏	❏
interpreting	❏	❏
reflecting	❏	❏

The ability to operate responsibly and effectively in small-group discussions is highly valued and recognized as a universally prized outcome expected from the educational system. Successful small-group discussions don't just happen, however; they develop as a result of careful planning, positive coaching, and lots of practice. By regularly having discussions in pairs and in groups of three, four, or more, students can develop the interactive skills necessary to share and build on the foundation of one another's interests, backgrounds, experiences, and insights.

Regardless of student age or ability, the subject area, or the nature or content of their discussions, the set of cooperative learning skills remains the same. For teachers, the process intrinsically cuts across disciplines and demonstrates how their joint responsibility for a set of skills and an outcome can be transferred from class to class, with opportunities for practice and evaluation provided. Whether the structure of the unit is interdisciplinary, multidisciplinary, or isolated within one subject area, cooperative learning strategies integrate and propel the learning process.

Setting Up Groups

To fully understand concepts, students need to toss out and test ideas or think aloud in their own informal spontaneous way. Students need frequent opportunities to discuss with someone else what they're reading, viewing, writing, listening to, observing, representing, thinking, or doing. These interactions might take place in pairs, in small groups, in combined groups, and, when appropriate, in large groups.

Groups need to be large enough to accommodate interaction and discussion, yet small enough to function efficiently without curbing spontaneity and independence. Although pairs and triads are often useful, depending on the task or objective, groups of four or five represent an optimal size. Such activities as finding solutions to mathematical problems or conducting experiments might best be handled in pairs or triads, for example, while discussions on controversial or complex issues in history or English might lend themselves to the optimum size. Groups larger than five require a more methodical, systematic structure and close supervision. The effort required to organize and maintain larger groups tends to detract from the ultimate benefits.

Small group membership can be determined by the teacher, by random design, or by the participants themselves. When teachers choose who works with whom, they usually do so for two reasons. Sometimes, they are attempting to redress some kind of perceived imbalance, such as exclusionary same-gender partnerships or constant equivalent-ability groupings. At other times, they are trying to avoid counterproductive situations, such as long-standing friendships interfering with group process.

Hard-and-fast rules, however, should be avoided. For some students, initially working with a friend or someone of similar ability may inject a needed sense of security and trust and encourage risk taking. On the other hand, some teachers worry about placing students of differing ability together, concerned that the more highly functioning student gains little from the partnership. The opposite is the case: in any mentoring situation, the mentor benefits most. Heterogeneous groupings also maximize a group's strengths while reflecting the diversity in which real-life collaboration occurs.

Clearly, teachers need to make their decisions about groupings based on their students' individual needs, abilities, and personalities. Some teachers begin the year by selecting all groupings themselves and, as students become more familiar with one another and comfortable in a variety of groupings, let students choose their own groupings. Other teachers begin with random or freely formed groups and intercede only as circumstances warrant. Whatever their approach, teachers should ensure that designated group membership is always varied. Group membership should never remain static.

Getting group discussion started doesn't have to be complicated or teacher dominated.

A simple, but effective method of creating random groups is to use colored, numbered, or lettered cards. The teacher decides how many students will constitute a group and how many groups will be necessary given the size of the class. If six groups of five are needed, the teacher makes up five red cards, five yellow cards, and so on until all the proposed groups are accounted for. The cards are shuffled and distributed randomly to the class. The teacher then designates areas within the classroom for each color and the groups are assembled. The teacher collects the cards to be reused when needed.

Depending on the constitution of the class, the students' experience with small-group learning, and the teacher's comfort level, students could devise their own groups based on criteria established beforehand. For example, teachers might set the number of friends allowed in a group or stipulate that there be an equal gender balance. In any event, they should plan to monitor these groups closely for proper group functioning. They should ensure that inclusive language, attitudes, and actions are observed and maintained at all times.

Individual members must have a good grasp of their roles in the group. They need to know what to do, reflect on how they perform at any one time and over a period of time, and set attainable, specific goals to improve their performances. This kind of knowledgeable, focused interaction develops slowly and with lots of practice and guidance.

Long before that happens, though, a teacher must organize groups and generate structured, useful discussion on a specific topic. Getting group discussion started doesn't have to be complicated or teacher dominated. If groups apply a simple protocol, discussions bloom. In one technique, a topic, issue, problem, or question is presented to the groups. Each member of a group must then express a personal reaction, thought, concern, or additional question. No one else in the group may make any remark about what has been said or begin interacting until everyone has had an opportunity to contribute. A member may "pass" momentarily, but must make a contribution when everyone else has finished. The key to this technique is that the discussion doesn't begin until everyone has had a chance to say something. Once everyone has spoken, however briefly, the floor is open to anyone to carry the discussion forward.

In another version of this technique, one group member acts as scribe while each group member asks a question about the subject, issue, or problem that he or she would like answered. The questions are written down and the group addresses these questions one by one. All questions left unanswered are offered to the larger class group and the teacher for consideration.

Brainstorming is, of course, a mainstay of group discussions. Although most people understand the term, the procedure involved varies considerably. The technique is designed to generate a list of examples, ideas, or questions to illustrate, expand on, or explore a central idea or topic. The following points can be used to guide the groups in their deliberations:

- Record all ideas.
- Don't evaluate ideas during collection.
- Quantity of ideas is important.
- Expanding on suggestions of others is encouraged.
- "Zany" ideas are welcomed.

After the brainstorming session, groups can discuss, evaluate, and prioritize suggestions to find their top three or five items. Each group works on chart paper with marker to allow results to be posted around the room for further discussion. In the reassembled, large-class grouping, students can be directed to find common elements from all the charts and challenged to offer suggestions that have come to mind after viewing the results.

Discussion Caveats

All sorts of odd, small-group practices masquerade under the name of cooperative learning.

Find out right at the beginning the kinds of experiences your students have had with small-group discussions. The more experienced they are, the less you may have to focus on process skills. Just because they're used to taking part in cooperative learning groups in previous years, however, is no guarantee that their skills are finely honed. All sorts of odd, small-group practices masquerade under the name of cooperative learning, and considerable readjustment and relearning may be in order. Although process skills need to be developed, the vehicle for refining them should remain front and centre. The topic under discussion should never be neglected. Here are a few caveats to bear in mind.

- Don't ask students to transcribe the course of a discussion.
  That kind of activity is usually assigned as a test of how well students were following and contributing to the discussion. As well as undercutting and devaluing the discussion itself, this practice forces students into needless duplication. Eventually, the attitude in the group becomes "the less we say, the less we have to write."
- Don't treat discussions as rehearsals for essay writing.
  A discussion is a complete learning experience in itself. If students realize that they will have to write down the arguments they're discussing, they cut the discussions off as quickly as possible to get on with the "real" task. Some students even remove themselves from the discussion and complete the written component instead. If you plan to have students write an essay after the discussion, the purpose for that discussion becomes preparation for writing. In that case, the discussion will centre on brainstorming, webbing, and other pre-writing activities.
- Don't ask students to report on other students in terms of either what they say or how they behave.
  Cooperative learning operates on a basis of trust and respect. If a group is operating poorly, other techniques can be implemented to turn the experience into a positive learning opportunity.

- Don't allow group process to be subverted.

  Working in groups doesn't automatically ensure that students are working effectively. If a group were given the task of reading a chapter in a text and answering questions based on that reading, for example, members might combine their efforts by splitting up the reading or by copying the answers from the better readers. If the goal was to maximize comprehension of the material, group members, at best, would come away with a fragmented understanding. The same effect results when members of a group divide math questions between them or opt to complete a project like a jigsaw puzzle, each member producing an isolated piece of the whole. In situations like these, a student's understandable goal of minimizing work through a group structure undermines the teacher's goal of maximizing learning.

Focusing on Discussion Skills

These skills can be taught and learned; in a classroom setting, they can also be evaluated.

The way that talk is skillfully and consciously applied in group situations determines how effective the learning will be. The individual who dominates a group with talk is undermining group process as much as the individual who says nothing: both lack essential discussion skills. However, these skills can be taught and learned; in a classroom setting, they can also be evaluated.

In *Learning to Work in Groups*, Matthew Miles identifies five functions that allow groups to perform effectively and which each group member, at various times, must fulfill. When group members accept the responsibility for fulfilling these functions, the group operates efficiently.

To be effective and responsible contributors to a small-group discussion, students need to become aware of the different roles they have to play in a group and be given opportunities to practise them. For each role, specific, reinforcing behaviors can be identified and defined. By practising and refining these behaviors, students can improve their effectiveness in small-group discussions. The key small-group discussion roles are as follows:

- sharing with others
- replying to others
- leading others
- supporting others
- evaluating the group's progress

Introduce students to each of these roles one by one and give them opportunities to practise one set of skills before focusing on another. Posting the skills in the classroom is an effective way of demonstrating how valued they are. Students should also have their own lists for reference.

The student guideline on page 90 highlights the five roles and the behaviors that identify the responsibilities of each.

Students need opportunities to reflect on how well their small-group discussion skills are developing. Before a peer discussion, for example, you might highlight one of the roles and point out specific actions they can take to refine their skills, for example, sharing with others. After the discussion, ask students to reflect on and write about whether or not they practised those skills, how well they succeeded or why they didn't, and what they would do in future to improve their

How to Develop Small-Group Discussion Skills

During discussions, I will share with others in my group by

- freely offering my opinions, feelings, or special knowledge in an effort to further group progress;
- listening carefully so I can link up what I know to what they know;
- giving facts and reasons to support my opinions.

During discussions, I will reply effectively to others in my group by

- listening carefully so that I can ask clarifying questions or make clarifying statements;
- responding freely to other people's questions, interests, problems, and concerns;
- sharing equally in the talking.

During discussions, I will show leadership in my group by

- suggesting my own ideas, other ways to solve problems, or new directions for the group to explore in an effort to keep the group headed in the right direction;
- speaking up without cutting someone off or without impeding the progress the group is making;
- offering suggestions without dominating the group.

During discussions, I will support others in my group by

- helping another person have his or her turn to speak;
- speaking without cutting off another person or too abruptly changing the subject;
- indicating in my gestures, facial expressions, or my postures that I'm interested in what is being said;
- giving people credit when they deserve it, even if they disagree with me.

During discussions, I will evaluate my group's progress by

- indicating whether or not I agree with ideas and decisions and expressing my reasons for taking that position;
- considering how well the group is working and how I might help the group work even more effectively;
- re-examining my own opinions and decisions and adjusting them when someone comes up with better ideas.

performance in that particular role. Remind them to comment only on their own performance, not that of a peer.

Student journals would be an ideal forum for these kinds of reflections. Over time, the response journal entries will present you with a profile of each student's involvement in group discussions, the degree to which a student is developing self-awareness, the personal goals a student sets, and the kind of success a student is finding in this area. You can compare each student's observations with your own perceptions and discuss them with the students one-on-one.

With younger students, written responses should either be tailored for their stage of readiness or eliminated. Having a discussion about everyone talking during small-group work, for example, is enough to focus students on sharing as one important aspect of group process. Regardless of the age group, developing, refining, and maintaining effective group skills is a complex process that evolves over a lifetime. Each step in the process, however small, is important.

Too many teachers assess small-group interactions merely in terms of individual demeanor or group results. In a classroom setting, discussion skills will develop only if they're evaluated both formatively and summatively. The next instrument, on page 92, illustrates one way to help students reflect on their own performances in a group and set goals for their next discussion. A summative evaluation marks sheet, shown under "Identifying Your Intentions," on page 53, in Chapter 3, demonstrates how marks can be assigned for the application of discussion skills.

Practising Small-Group Discussion Skills

(Please place a check mark beside each skill you practised this period.)

During this discussion, I was able to

- ask a question ❏
- ask for an explanation of what someone meant ❏
- check to see if someone else understood ❏
- add to someone else's idea ❏
- get the group back to work ❏
- keep track of the time ❏
- share information or an idea ❏
- restate something to make it clearer ❏
- congratulate someone for something said or done ❏
- disagree without hurting someone's feelings ❏
- encourage someone ❏
- support someone ❏
- invite someone else to talk ❏
- keep the discussion orderly and friendly ❏
- share my feelings ❏
- give my viewpoint ❏

During our next discussion, I will try to practise these three skills:

1. _____

2. _____

3. _____

The Search for Meaning

We're all meaning-making machines: we can't help ourselves. We're driven to make sense of everything around us. We discover familiar shapes in clouds, recognize patterns in the stars, and uncover harmony of composition in an autumn forest. Every day is filled with untold mysteries to investigate. We hear a faint rustling in a darkened closet and we have to identify the source; we smell an unfamiliar aroma and we wonder what it is; we see flashing lights and cars slowing down on the highway ahead, and we begin to formulate possible causes.

Language is an intrinsic part of this meaning-making process. Politics and religion fuel endless informal debates anywhere, anytime. We probe our relationships, solve problems, and resolve conflict with talk. We're constantly trying to make sense of our experiences, real or vicarious, through discourse. Try coming out of a movie theatre, for example, without talking to your companions about the controversial film you've just seen. Unlike talk in the classroom, however, we don't insist that everyone speak in sentences or enunciate clearly and distinctly. All we ask is that people make sense when they talk.

When we write to think, we treat our writing just like our talking. Nobody worries unduly about their spelling or grammatical correctness as they try to unravel and express profound feelings and beliefs in their personal journals. Handwriting and standard usage are minor concerns to a manager jotting down some thoughts on an envelope prior to an impromptu speech. A physician making notes about a patient's symptoms and attempting to discern a pattern is as oblivious to mechanical correctness as a poet exploring, in a tattered scribbler, the relationship between majestic mountains and urban, concrete towers. They're all focused on the function, not the form.

Once we learn how to read, we can't stop ourselves: we're constantly reading our surroundings. Try sitting alone in front of a desk in someone else's office and not reading upside down the papers scattered on the surface. We're not nosy — we're just readers attracted to words much as iron filings are attracted to a magnet. Try ignoring billboards or the slogans on the side of a passing bus. How many times have you read the designer's name on an article of clothing? Why do many of us read the newspaper day after day? And why do we never need a list of comprehension questions to make sense of it all?

Learning that uses language is an entirely different process from learning a language itself. When teachers are structuring and then evaluating learning experiences, they need to keep that difference in mind. Outside the classroom, our need to make sense of the world is instinctive and reflexive. Inside the classroom, unless we're careful, language and learning begin to work at cross-purposes. If students believe that their language output is a product on display, not a means to an end, they will focus on fluency at the expense of meaning.

Young children instinctively know how to use language for learning. They use all their senses to explore and figure out their world and language becomes one more "sense." A new toy is touched, regarded, smelled, tasted, shaken, and listened to; when they acquire language, children talk, write, and read about it.

The conception of language as an additional tool to apply to the daily task of learning can be easily blunted. In the classroom, we need to keep the language floodgates open and utilize language's power. When language flows unimpeded, so does learning.

5

The Reflection Conundrum

"I'd like to take more of a leadership role in the school, but I'm not sure where to start."
"I'm not sure how much of what goes on outside my classroom door is my responsibility."
"I know that the school should be more effective, but I can't make that happen alone."

No two schools are ever alike.

Usually based on a school board's own version, a school vision statement contains the fundamental and guiding principles that support, shape, and direct why and how people act and interact within the environment. As a foundational belief statement, the vision determines the manner in which the curriculum is implemented in your classroom and throughout the school.

A vision statement describes an ideal state, however. Each year, school administrators confront such shifting variables as clients, program, budget, staff, and even the condition of the school building. They also have their own ideas about how a school should function, as do the teachers and the members of the community. Is it any wonder that the unified approach to education exemplified by curricular documents is interpreted so differently from school to school and from classroom to classroom?

Adaptability and variability produce unique school cultures: no two schools are ever alike. Only when teachers are embedded in a strained, uncomfortable, or stressful school environment, however, do they usually consider the values reflected in the school culture and the effect of those values on their own classrooms. Any dissonance between the values inherent in a classroom and those of the school at large can have serious repercussions.

Depending on the age of their students and the timetable, some teachers attempt to "cocoon" their classrooms. Ignoring what's going on in other classrooms or around the school, they try to create a safe, positive, and enriching space within the classroom's four walls.

Unfortunately, those walls aren't hermetically sealed.

Any time students come into contact with other teachers, students from other classrooms, or administrators, anywhere in or around the building, they also walk headlong into a potential clash of values. From the rotary teacher who abhors talking in the classroom, to the teacher on hall duty who ignores the constant bullying to the vice-principal who seems reluctant to enforce school rules, other people can seriously undermine the values intrinsic to an effective learning/teaching environment.

Schools are subject to constant change. Teaching is as cyclical as the seasons and as varied as the weather. Staff, students, and political priorities change, year by year, and with them, the dynamics that energize and define a school's character.

Contrary to common wisdom, teachers understand and expect change.

Contrary to common wisdom, teachers understand and expect change. That's why they're so successful at filtering out any change with which they do not agree. They realize that each September brings new challenges from a new set of students, possibly a new administrator and a new curriculum, and maybe even a new grade level. They expect the hurdles, glitches, and inconveniences that can mar a school environment, and they expect administration to exhort them to jump on the next educational bandwagon. In response, they fall back onto the routines and practices that work in their own classrooms. They focus on controlling their own small patches of turf, and hope that order, goodwill, and unity will eventually prevail throughout the building.

That foxhole mentality isn't enough to protect teachers and their classes or to achieve the desired classroom environment. What if your classroom isn't operating the way it should and the fault lies with the school? How do you go about finding out what's wrong? What if the school isn't operating the way it should and you're not quite sure what you can do about it? If you find yourself at an ineffective school, your integrity demands that you make one of these two choices: to fight for positive change from within or to look elsewhere for a school environment more supportive of your beliefs and methods.

The first step is determining just what your school's culture is. You can do that through a review of established fundamental values and a fresh focus on the nature of various partnerships.

Reviewing Fundamental Values

When we define curriculum as everything that happens in a school, we're acknowledging that it doesn't end at the classroom door. For a school to function effectively, certain fundamental values have to be recognized and consistently implemented by everyone in the building. The foundation of any curriculum rests on cooperation for the good of all and respect for self and peers. All students need to feel safe in the environment and valued by their peers and by adults; all teachers need to feel safe in the environment and valued by their peers and by the administration. Everyone needs to feel positive about themselves and their abilities and to feel that they are engaged in worthwhile, productive activities.

As you consider the following fundamentals, think in terms of students first and then apply the fundamentals to your own professional context. A classroom or a school structured to maximize learning potential will include the components outlined below.

An environment free of sexist, racial, cultural, ability, and homophobic stereotyping

An insistence on equity helps lay the foundation for a learning/teaching environment inhospitable to discrimination and harassment. In this environment, all adults serve as examples of positive behavior, displaying, for example, a genuine courtesy toward others and a respect for individual differences. In language and in actions, teachers consistently display inclusive values — double standards are corrosive and insidious. Adults interact with one another and with students in a fair, respectful, and equitable manner. Administrators set the tone for teachers, and both set the tone for students.

Regard for the learning of and respect for others in the class

All students have the right to learn and all students have the right to respect.

All students have the right to learn and all students have the right to respect. Regardless of disability, gender, sexual orientation, race, ethnocultural origin, faith, or socio-economic status, all students must be empowered to learn through positive reinforcement, the understanding and acceptance of individual differences, and the encouragement of trial and error. Mistakes, especially, must be welcomed and affirmed as an authentic component of the learning process.

Time for students to learn cooperatively in pairs and in small groups

As discussed in Chapter 4, cooperative learning refers to a range of small-group instructional techniques focusing on peer collaboration. Cooperative learning strategies, in and of themselves, have been shown to contribute to higher academic achievement, to increase self-esteem, to improve social skills, and to facilitate language development. In addition, teachers who hope to counter bias, discrimination, and bigotry of all kinds need to make these techniques a mainstay of their programs.

Administrators, as well, need to value and encourage the use of cooperative learning strategies throughout the school and apply them themselves as they interact with and mentor teachers.

Opportunities for students to make decisions and solve problems related to the classroom experience

Students who are constantly reacting to decisions that others make for them have difficulty assuming responsibility for whatever happens as a result of those decisions. If the teacher makes the rules, enforcing the rules is the teacher's problem alone. When students take active part in the decision-making process, however, they have a vested interest in maintaining the integrity of those decisions. As a result, they are more apt to accept responsibility for the interactions that occur in their environment. Self- and peer-evaluation — especially formative evaluation — are also essential growth activities.

Learning is essentially a problem-solving activity. As students attempt to make sense of and cope with the world, they learn. The more that activities in the classroom can be placed in a problem-solving structure, the more those activities become meaningful for the students.

Opportunities for teachers to make decisions and solve problems related to the school-wide experience

Teachers also have to examine the decision-making processes in their school. They should take active part in how issues involving program, budget, staffing, or health and safety, for instance, are handled. Rubber-stamping decisions made elsewhere is not enough. Ideally, they would feel empowered to assist in setting a school's goals, not frustrated by policies handed down from above.

A degree of independent choice and responsibility for what, when, and how the individual learns

Knowing how to make good choices is an essential life skill and one that will develop only when real opportunities to make choices are provided. The classroom program needs to be flexible enough to recognize and match individual needs, interests, and learning styles. Texts, teaching pace, learning/teaching techniques, and related follow-up activities should be treated as variables that can be adapted when necessary to suit individual needs. One size seldom fits all. As well, when students are able to select program components, such as topics, modes of presentation, or optional credits, they can help design an optimal learning path for their individual profiles. They can also assume greater responsibility for their individual learning outcomes.

Keep in mind, however, that making good choices is a skill acquired over time. If unfortunate choices are made, they can be turned into learning opportunities. Students accustomed to making choices regularly and without risk make choices that are mature and effective.

Time for students to reflect on what and how they are learning

Teaching without reflection is like treading water indefinitely — sooner or later your head will go under.

Language and learning are intrinsically linked. To fully understand ideas, students need the chance to pick away at them. They need to "think aloud" in informal talk or writing.

Reflection is the soul of the learning process. Students need the opportunity and freedom to mull over ideas in a personally significant manner. Doing this will allow them to internalize what these ideas mean and how they relate to their own lives. Individual student-teacher conferences and small-group, cooperative learning strategies assist in the process. Response journals, as well, allow students beyond the primary grades to reflect in writing on their learning across the curriculum.

For teachers themselves, the hectic and nerve-wracking pace of day-to-day teaching pushes reflection into a tomorrow that never seems to arrive; however, teaching without reflection is like treading water indefinitely — sooner or later your head will go under.

This chapter is devoted to helping teachers reflect on the state of their own teaching and their schools, and to set goals pertaining to professional growth.

Gaining Perspective on Partnerships

Teachers often feel beleaguered, under attack, and on the defensive.

A complete vision for an effective, flourishing classroom and school requires one more component: a belief in and absolute commitment to the concept of collaboration. Most teachers, including administrators, admire the notion that they must create working partnerships with their colleagues; their clients, the students; and their clients' parents and guardians. They like the idea, but they have difficulty turning the belief into practice. Although teachers believe in collaborative, inclusive school cultures, they too often slip into a beleaguered fortress mentality.

The sense of isolation sets in when teachers are closeted alone all day, day after day, with the full and constant responsibility for a class of young people weighing on their shoulders. Arranging for an unscheduled washroom break can be a major undertaking. The pressure of always being on display, on duty, and tied to a room and an invariable, impersonal schedule can be demoralizing. Although the school is filled with other teachers who understand what they're going through, that sympathy offers cold comfort. Teachers spend most of their time separated from their colleagues. The hope for collegiality and collaboration often gives way to a feeling of being all alone together.

Education is also an inescapably political profession. Such issues as standardized test scores, salary negotiations, and curriculum reviews are discussed and evaluated in a public forum and are subject to political agendas. Teachers often feel beleaguered, under attack, and on the defensive — their relationship with the public can verge on the adversarial. For their part, parents are often subject to conflict between their own impressionistic, sometimes turbulent school memories, the frequently critical public spotlight on teaching and teachers, and their specific, personal relationships with teachers. Not surprisingly, teachers are often torn between avoiding the public's jaundiced view of education and cultivating the open, trusting dialogue with parents and guardians that will illuminate understanding of their charges.

Regardless of the problematic circumstances, parents must not be left on the outside looking in. Individual teachers and parents and guardians must continue to forge their necessary partnerships. An effective collaboration with parents and guardians, however, can occur only when they are completely informed, consulted often, and recognized as equally responsible partners in their children's learning experiences.

When you look closely, the interests and concerns of teachers, parents, and students remain notably alike.

Each year, the teacher wonders:

- What will my students be like?
- Can we keep the school safe?
- Will I have trouble with any of the parents?
- How large will the classes be?
- Will I be able to teach them everything they'll need to know?
- How many of my students will have special needs? What will they be?
- Will the new principal (or department head) help or hinder what I want to do?
- Will there be money in the budget for the books and equipment I need?
- What's the next bandwagon we're supposed to jump on?

Each year, the parent or guardian wonders:

- What will the teacher be like?
- Is the school safe?
- Will my child have trouble with any of the teachers?
- How large will the classes be?
- Will my child be taught what she or he needs to know?
- Will the school accommodate my child's special needs?
- Will the principal (or department head) welcome my help or think I'm meddling?
- Will the school have the necessary and appropriate books and equipment?
- What bandwagon will the school be jumping on this year?

Each year the student wonders:

- What will the teacher be like?
- Will the school be safe?
- Will I have trouble with any of the teachers or any of the other students?
- How large will my classes be?
- Will I be able to learn everything I'm supposed to learn?
- Will I get help if I need it?
- How strict will the principal, vice-principals, and teachers be?
- Will I be able to understand the textbooks?
- What new things will we have to do this year that the school has never done before?

Evaluation always drives a wedge between collaborators.

Teachers take the first step toward building partnerships by creating collaborative, inclusive cultures in their own classrooms. As trusted mentors, they demonstrate, or model, the values that underpin the process of meaningful learning, presenting learning as a multi-faceted, open-ended activity in which adults and students take part for a variety of reasons and in a variety of ways. In that same role, teachers maintain a continuing dialogue with their students, supporting, advising, guiding, explaining, and directing as the need arises.

Evaluation, however, always drives a wedge between collaborators. Teachers give tests; students take them. Teachers write report cards; parents and guardians read them.

Teachers need to recognize and constantly try to bridge the gaps imposed by their role as evaluators. As compassionate supervisors, then, teachers should design an evaluation system that reinforces rather than disenfranchises the student learners. Implicit in such an evaluation system is respect for an individual's mode of expression, regardless of how tentative or untutored that expression might be. Although sophistication of expression can be recognized, the focus rests primarily on the learning itself. Within an inclusive evaluation system, teachers monitor how well their students are learning, discover ways to diagnose their needs, and help students develop solutions to their own problems.

Reporting to parents and guardians can too easily become something where form supersedes function: teachers report at prescribed times and in a prescribed manner, usually in a set number of report cards and interviews each year. In this model, parents and students alike learn to dread the ritualistic judgments handed down by the teachers on high.

Inclusive teachers, on the other hand, aim to establish a more interdependent relationship with their parents and guardians. They contact the home whenever they have questions or concerns about a student's progress or welfare to alert the adults at home and also to enlist their assistance and advice. They also use phone calls and written notes to provide positive feedback whenever students deserve to be congratulated. The more teachers are able to include parents and guardians in the day-to-day course of events, the more all the adults involved can operate as a team for the students' benefit.

Collaboration has a snowball effect. When teachers earn the trust and respect of their students, the trust and respect of their parents and guardians will follow. As they learn to find the time necessary to allow collegiality to flourish, teachers will discover that those peer relationships feed back into and enrich their primary collaborations with students and their parents and guardians.

But the clearest of visions, the strongest of principles, and the best of intentions aren't enough. You may know where you want to go, but you still have to figure out how to get there. If you hold in your mind an image of your ideal classroom, you still need the pragmatic nuts and bolts and functional know-how to turn that image into reality.

The true challenge of teaching lies in recognizing and managing the constraints.

The Need to Evaluate Your School

Change in schools is often difficult for the wrong reasons.

One of the major constraints on teaching may be the school culture. Teachers are not just busy. Along with managing their daily and constant multi-tasking, they struggle against innumerable roadblocks. These may range from incompetent administrators and inadequate resources to cognitively inappropriate curriculum and politically motivated, narrow, and prescriptive evaluation systems.

The best quality that teachers possess is their determination to make things work for all their students. Even if a government were to decide, for example, that students in Grade 1 needed to learn the Theory of Relativity, primary teachers would likely stand on their heads trying to help their students find some image of the theory that they could understand. Teachers remain determined to find a way.

Having said that, though, it's true that teachers need to take an objective and critical look at their school cultures. They need to determine how many of the problems they face can be attributed to or exacerbated by forces outside their control.

Teachers themselves might be eager to implement a change in their programs, but the predominant school culture might determine otherwise. In any school, "going it alone" is like swimming upstream against a heavy current. When the swimmer gets worn down, the current takes control.

Change in schools is often difficult for the wrong reasons. Teachers, possibly the principal or vice-principal, parents, or even some of the students may balk at anything other than the accustomed way of doing things. Instead of making a decision based on reflective practice, they may convince themselves that because something, such as using spellers and grammar texts, has always been done, then it is clearly the right way. They may also undermine a new initiative, such as a strict code of behavior, through poor communication or unfair application, making it an uphill battle to establish a safe, orderly, and equitable classroom environment. Principals, especially, can be ambivalent about change. They tend to rail against the unwillingness of teachers to embrace change while carefully ensuring that no one on staff "makes waves."

Only when teachers fully understand the problematic areas in their schools are they able to set realistic goals for their classrooms. The more ineffective the school culture, the more difficult it is to manage a classroom; the more effective the school culture, the more classroom values and routines are reinforced and reaffirmed throughout the building. In the first situation, a sense of "us" against "them" prevails and staff morale is low; in the second, teachers feel empowered in a culture that constantly builds dynamic partnerships among teachers, students, and parents.

Given this context, before you examine your own teaching behaviors and accept responsibility for improving your own techniques, take an objective and critical look at your school's culture. Regardless of location, size, budget, or socio-economic factors, some schools are effective and others less so. They differ only in the manner in which they are managed. Classroom teachers need to know how their school stacks up. Here are specific questions to answer:

- How effective is my school's culture?
- How is the school culture having an impact on my classroom?
- What aspects of the school culture need to change?
- What needs to be done to effect those changes?
- Who is responsible for the change process?
- What is the prognosis for effective change?

Be sure to take a good, hard look at your school culture.

The following reflection tool points to answers to those questions by honing in on the discrete items and characteristics that distinguish effective and ineffective schools. Based on persuasive research into the nature of effective schools, it is divided into five areas: discipline, instruction, collaboration, parental involvement, and evaluation. This artificial separation allows each component to be highlighted, but ignores the connections between and among the various areas. For example, instruction directly affects the kind and amount of discipline needed in a classroom just as the consistency and quality of discipline in a school directly affects classroom instruction. In actual practice and in similar ways, all of the five areas are intimately interrelated.

The reflection tool lets you explicitly identify your school's strengths and weaknesses. In the area of collaboration, for example, you can quickly discern how much peer and administrative support you can expect as you plan, prepare, and implement your programs. In the same way, the section on discipline will underscore systemic problems that will inevitably affect your classroom environment.

Be sure to take a good, hard look at your school culture. Once you have done so, you may be ready to tackle specific school-wide and classroom challenges — or to head for the nearest exit.

School Assessment Reflection Tool

In this reflection tool, please indicate the extent to which you agree or disagree that each statement describes the dominant behavior in your school.

1 = strongly disagree   2 = disagree   3 = agree   4 = strongly agree

Discipline

- Administration communicates high expectations for behavior and clear consequences for disruptive or negative behavior.

  1   2   3   4

- Staff communicates high expectations for behavior and clear consequences for disruptive or negative behavior.

  1   2   3   4

- Rules are clearly communicated to all and reinforced using the same, simple, easily understood language.

  1   2   3   4

- Dangerous or disruptive behavior is never tolerated.

  1   2   3   4

- Administration enforces a code of conduct in a fair, consistent, and equitable manner.

  1   2   3   4

- A safe, orderly, and equitable environment is enforced throughout the school.

  1   2   3   4

- Staff displays a respectful attitude toward students.

  1   2   3   4

- Students display a respectful attitude toward one another.

  1   2   3   4

- Teachers are on time for their supervisory duties.

  1   2   3   4

- Teachers accept responsibility for supervising all students anywhere in the building or on school grounds.

  1   2   3   4

Instruction

- Teachers believe that their efforts will affect how well students learn.

  1   2   3   4

- Teachers clearly communicate that all students can and are expected to learn.

  1   2   3   4

- In addition to mandated requirements, teachers willingly spend extra time beyond the school day on preparation and planning.

  1   2   3   4

- Teachers believe that students with special needs should be integrated into regular programs.

  1   2   3   4

- Teachers use cooperative learning strategies.

  1   2   3   4

- Teachers modify or adapt instruction to suit students' needs.

  1   2   3   4

- Teachers make learning relevant to a student's background, culture, and previous learning experiences.

  1   2   3   4

- Class sizes are reasonable.

  1   2   3   4

- Students are withdrawn from classes only with ample notice.

  1   2   3   4

- Frivolous announcements or similar classroom interruptions are frowned upon.

  1   2   3   4

- Administration encourages research-based instruction.

  1   2   3   4

- Ample time is scheduled in all classes for in-class reading (as opposed to question answering or related follow-up activities).

  1   2   3   4

Collaboration

- Administration and staff work together as a mutually supportive team.

    1   2   3   4

- The principal functions as the instructional leader.

    1   2   3   4

- Teachers willingly share resources, supplies, and ideas.

    1   2   3   4

- Teachers meet to discuss the progress of students they share.

    1   2   3   4

- Teachers plan, prepare, and deliver lessons as a team with the teacher-librarian or other teachers.

    1   2   3   4

- Teachers meet regularly with other teachers of the same grade or division and believe such meetings are worthwhile components of their programs.

    1   2   3   4

- Teachers meet regularly for subject-specific discussions and planning and believe such meetings are worthwhile components of their programs.

    1   2   3   4

- Professional development is encouraged and accommodated within the school day.

    1   2   3   4

- Teachers are consulted on how best to spend the school budget.

    1   2   3   4

- Teachers are consulted on timetable priorities.

    1   2   3   4

- Teachers are consulted when developing school curricular priorities.

    1   2   3   4

- Teachers have significant input into setting the agenda for staff meetings.

    1   2   3   4

- Special events, such as concerts or play days, are well organized and run.

    1   . 2   3   4

Parental involvement

- Parents are informed of school events through frequent, jargon-free newsletters in their own language.

  1   2   3   4

- Parent volunteers work in the library daily.

  1   2   3   4

- Parent volunteers work in classrooms daily.

  1   2   3   4

- Parent volunteers are involved in such activities as excursions, fund raising, and special events.

  1   2   3   4

- The school hosts informational workshops for parents on such topics as literacy, homework, and health issues.

  1   2   3   4

- The school embraces a vibrant, enthusiastic, and active parent-teacher association.

  1   2   3   4

- Parents and selected staff and school administrators meet regularly.

  1   2   3   4

Evaluation

- Administration monitors and assesses program effectiveness in a variety of formal and informal ways.

  1   2   3   4

- Teachers systematically assess their own programs in a formative manner.

  1   2   3   4

- Teachers systematically assess student progress in a formative manner.

  1   2   3   4

- Summative and formative student evaluation occur regularly and frequently using a wide range of assessment techniques and instruments.

  1   2   3   4

- All evaluative data is used to direct program modifications.

    1   2   3   4

- Parents are informed about their children's progress in a variety of formal and informal ways.

    1   2   3   4

- Parents are consulted and involved in planning and implementing remedial programs and approaches for their children.

    1   2   3   4

- Students believe that their success in school is related to how hard they work.

    1   2   3   4

The patterns that emerge from this survey are more instructive than the raw scores. If you find that you agree or strongly agree with most of the items in most of the categories, you can feel reassured that you're part of an effectively functioning school environment. If you mostly disagree or strongly disagree with many of the items in several of the categories, you'll have a clear idea whether and how the school environment may be having an impact on your classroom; you'll also see how to focus your efforts toward positive change. If two of the categories are instruction and discipline, however, change may be slow to come and difficult to achieve. Should you find that you disagree or strongly disagree with most of the items in most of the categories, you will clearly understand the magnitude of the problem and the small probability of a successful change process.

Most teachers will find that they are in schools that are neither completely effective nor totally ineffective. Their school environments, consequently, will both support and limit the effectiveness of their own classroom teaching. Weak areas will be magnified and strengths muted. The limitations imposed by the ineffective areas of a school's culture, as well, tend to wear down a staff's best intentions and erode teachers' inherent passion for their profession.

Passion for teaching will often tip the balance.

When teachers lose their passion for teaching and begin going through the motions only, they are, at best, neutralized and, at worst, paralyzed. Passion for teaching will often tip the balance from a day heading into the dumpster to a day filled with promise and satisfaction. Passion for a subject, a topic, or a concept can touch and intrigue even the most disinterested of students; passion will ensure that teachers keep their students safe, keep students feeling good about themselves, and keep students involved in worthwhile learning programs; passion will also engender a sense of purpose and mission, uniting colleagues and parents in a spirit of collaboration. Finally, passion will help teachers discover those moments of humor and sheer zaniness that can restore perspective and brighten the darkest of days.

Considering the Influence of School Cultures

Before teachers begin to either work toward positive change in identified areas or look outside their current schools, they need to understand the cultural values that underlie their professional lives. Becoming actively aware of the influence of school culture, past and present, is necessary if they are to move on in their efforts to contribute to the development of an effective school.

The compelling influence of a school's culture on the behavior of teachers is seldom recognized. Critics who demand change in schools, politicians who mandate change, and administrators who implement change continue to treat teachers either as data discs that can be wiped clean and reprogrammed at will or faulty automobiles under recall for design flaws. They don't realize that the forces of acculturation that mould most teachers are impervious to outside conditioning. Teachers will change their methods significantly only if they believe it's the right thing to do. They make that decision gradually, in the context of their present teaching assignments and past experiences, and through an intensive, self-directed process of collaboration. The schools where teachers are now have everything to do both with the kind of teachers they are now and the kind of teachers they may become.

The two major influences shaping teachers have nothing to do with teacher training, specialized courses, in-servicing, directives, guidelines, or mandated policies. The majority of teachers will teach as they were taught when they were students or in the manner of their first professional colleagues. People either come to the profession already knowing the kind of teacher they want to be or, through the culture of their first school, they learn what kind of teacher they should be. Despite the noise and bustle of the latest educational initiative or the proud trumpeting of critics, politicians, and administrators, teachers, by and large, continue to go about their business much as they always have, guided and influenced by their past and present mentors.

These influences can be as diverse as they are arbitrary.

The models supplied by their own teachers offer teachers-to-be a smorgasbord of approaches from which to choose. If, as students, prospective teachers mainly encountered authoritarian lecturers, they may enter the profession expecting to fulfill that role. They may have learned that teachers spend most of their time assigning and marking written assignments, or engaging their students in hands-on investigations, or adopting a laisser-faire approach to student behavior. They will likely try to emulate those teachers with characteristics they admire or with whom they formed a bond or found success.

The culture of a teacher's first school or of any school new to a teacher can be equally potent in influence. Much like fresh raindrops falling into a free-flowing river, a torpid pond, or the open ocean, teachers are quickly subsumed by the dominant culture of their colleagues.

Schools, however, rarely manifest a single, homogeneous culture; a typical school will contain two, three, or more cliques comprised of teachers with similar beliefs, attitudes, and methods. For new or beginning teachers, whichever clique surrounds their classroom or dominates their grade or subject meetings is the one they will usually imitate. These influences are so powerful that even when teachers are withdrawn from a school for intensive in-servicing in an opposing viewpoint, they will revert once they're re-immersed in the school culture with which they identify.

For a beginning teacher or an experienced teacher new to a school, department, or grade, the process of acculturation follows a familiar pattern. Newcomers quiz their new colleagues in the adjoining classrooms, or in the same grade, or in their shared office about how this unfamiliar school culture operates. They ask questions like these:

- What does the principal, as well as other administrators, expect?
- What are they like?
- How supportive are they?
- What extra duties are required?
- What are the kids like?
- How tough do you have to be?
- What are the parents like?
- What content is covered and how is it delivered?
- What books are used?
- What kind of evaluation is used and how often are the reporting periods?

The established teachers answer all the questions, and quickly and efficiently show the newcomers the ropes. The process of acculturation has begun.

The culture of a teacher's first school or of any school new to a teacher can be equally potent in influence.

Making a Commitment to Reflection

Although experiences in schools past and present play a significant role in shaping teachers, they're not the whole story. Many other factors influence how people go about the business of teaching: their personal value systems, a passion for a particular subject area, an outgoing personality, a highly clinical, analytical nature, or a belief in social activism are among the myriad individual differences that might direct and personalize professional growth. That very individuality is a teacher's greatest strength: the unique attributes that individuals bring to a school culture can be the key to creating interdependence among teachers and can act as a catalyst for positive change.

But teachers are cautious about altering what they do and are wise to be so. They've been pushed onto too many stalled bandwagons and watched the pendulum of change swing back and forth too often. They realize that they are the ones who stabilize and anchor their ever-changing environments. Strong teachers monitor and assess everything that is happening around them and determine what is worthwhile and effective.

Teaching and reflection must go hand in hand.

Teaching and reflection must go hand in hand. A commitment to reflection is more a mindset than a strict or structured set of procedures. Teachers who make this commitment automatically review any significant interaction with students or peers in a simple and direct way. Whether it's a lesson they've just taught, a student they've disciplined, or a conflict they've experienced with a colleague, they apply a reflective mental checklist to the episode:

- What was I trying to accomplish?
- How successful was I?
- How do I feel about what I've done and the way I went about it?
- What kind of follow-up action do I need to take?

This kind of individual reflection spurs individual growth.

For change to occur in a school, though, teachers have to take part in a recurrent process of *shared* reflection: they have to collaborate. They can't isolate themselves in a school and expect to fulfill their responsibilities to students satisfactorily. What happens in other classrooms, in the hallways, in the lunchroom, and in the main office is *everyone's* business. Values are as crucial to learning as air is to breathing, and both circulate freely throughout a school.

When you begin to collaborate, you usually choose a neighboring colleague or two or three people in the same grade or subject area; some issues, on the other hand, demand a school-wide approach. Sometimes, you address a common problem, concern, or instructional unit; sometimes, you begin to reveal and discuss your philosophy of teaching. People have to find their own routes into collaboration.

Taking a collaborative approach to teaching isn't easy; it's both time consuming and demanding. When teachers reflect in groups, time is required to develop consensus on such questions as these:

- What are we trying to accomplish?
- What's the best way to go about it?
- How do we assess how effective we are?
- What are we learning about the way we're doing things?

Teachers also have to polish and practise a set of sophisticated, interactive skills if they hope to make their collaborative efforts worth their time. Openness and honesty are crucial. At times teachers need to share private opinions and experiences that they'd much rather keep to themselves, except by doing so they would limit the effectiveness of the group process. When others share in a similar fashion, they have to measure carefully how to reply; an ill-advised response can do untold damage to an individual's self-esteem and to the task at hand. Teachers also have to judge when to offer the group leadership and when to offer someone else support. Most difficult of all, they have to learn how to evaluate the group's progress and decide, if necessary, how best to intervene with the intent of furthering that progress.

This book has dealt in detail with how teachers can control their environment and reclaim their time. It has offered systems to manage the daily onslaught of secretarial, administrative, supervisory, and organizational tasks that teachers are expected to fulfill. Putting these systems in place should free teachers to engage in recurrent reflection. Once teachers can effectively deal with the minutiae, deadlines, frustrations, and disturbances that isolate them from their peers, they can direct time and energy to developing a community of learners. They can also restore perspective and improve their teaching practice through reflection.

In effective schools, teachers free themselves to collaborate, and through collaboration, they're empowered to learn — in many ways, the teacher should be seen as the "lead learner." Through their own experiences, teachers learn how to empower their students. Once that happens, the learning comes full circle.

The teacher should be seen as the "lead learner."

Appendices

Anecdotal Records

Student name: _____

Notation: _____

_____

Date: _____

Notation: _____

_____

Date: _____

Notation: _____

_____

Date: _____

Notation: _____

_____

Date: _____

Notation: _____

_____

Date: _____

Contact with Parent/Guardian

Student name: _____

Adult contact: _____

Date: _____

Type of contact: Check the appropriate box.

telephone to ❑   phone from ❑   interview ❑

written note to ❑   written note from ❑

agenda note to ❑   agenda note from ❑

Issue:

_____

_____

_____

Relevant details:

_____

_____

_____

Proposed action (if any):

_____

_____

Date action taken (if applicable): d ____   m ____   y 20____

Behavior Contract

Student: _____

Date: _____

Terms: _____

_____

_____

_____

_____

_____

Student signature: _____

Teacher witness: _____

The following section to be completed on _____

Terms of contract fulfilled: _____   Check one: Yes ❏   No ❏

Student comment: _____

_____

_____

_____

Teacher comment: _____

_____

_____

_____

Glossary

The definitions in this glossary are consistent with the meanings that are used in the text.

achievement the attainment of specific learning goals in a school setting

affective a term from psychology referring to emotional activity

at risk a descriptor applied to students with academic, emotional, or social difficulties or a combination of these serious enough to jeopardize acceptable progress in school

behaviorist focusing on observable behavior; also arranging learning experiences in scope and sequence and applying rewards and reviews to help students make successful, step-by-step progress

brainstorming generating a list of examples, ideas, or questions to illustrate, expand, or explore a central idea or topic (It is based on recording all ideas, not evaluating ideas during collecting, valuing quantity of ideas, encouraging students to expand on one another's ideas, and welcoming "zany" ideas.)

cognitive a term from psychology referring to intellectual activity

collaboration problem solving in pairs and in other small groups (see also **cooperative learning**)

comprehension acquiring the meaning of any kind of communication

conferencing opportunities to discuss ideas and problems in pairs or small groups; conferences can be conducted in a variety of formats with and without the teacher.

contract a written agreement with a student to formalize a change process

control disorders clinical conditions suffered by students who are unable to consistently monitor and regulate their own behavior

cooperative learning a variety of small-group instructional techniques focusing on peer collaboration

"cueing" response a guiding suggestion or hint that gives an individual a sense of the kinds of responses possible; the cue serves as an example or model. Individuals are encouraged to develop their own responses based on their own purposes for reading and their personal perspectives as independent readers.

curriculum at one time, a synonym for syllabus; the current definition, which reflects the complexity of learning, refers to everything that happens in a school.

desktop publishing using the resources of the personal computer to give individuals access to the publishing process; software ranges from simple word processing programs to sophisticated publishing programs offering a variety of text and graphic capabilities.

detention a form of punishment in a school in which an individual is detained and confined in a specific location during the school day

diagnostic evaluation an aspect of formative evaluation; becoming familiar with each student's interests, abilities, preferred learning style, and learning difficulties

diary (private) an in-class record of personal observations, random jottings, and thoughts and feelings; shared only if the student agrees

discipline the practice of establishing correct order and behavior in a classroom using such methods as rules, direct instruction, and punishment

drafting the recursive cycle of revising and editing written material

editing checking, prior to a final copy, for errors in spelling, usage, and clarity of expression

essay a relatively brief literary composition, usually in prose, giving the author's views on a particular topic

ethnocultural identifying with a group of people sharing a heritage and ancestry as well as other characteristics which might include physical, cultural, linguistic, or religious components

evaluation a process that determines progress toward and attainment of specific goals; assessing student progress and achievement as well as program effectiveness

exceptionalities physical, intellectual, social, or emotional characteristics that mark an individual's development as significantly different from the norm; this difference may signal either a gifted or deficient development.

exposition written material intended to explain, clarify, or define

fluency the ability to speak, write, or read aloud smoothly, easily, and with clear expression of ideas; with independent reading, it has come to mean reading with mechanical competency and mature understanding.

formative evaluation the ongoing assessment of student progress aimed almost exclusively at assisting learning and at improving the educational experience; geared to an individual's needs and personal growth

grammar a study of the patterns of word formation in a language and the structure of word order in sentences, clauses, and phrases

heterogeneous including in an instructional group students of varying abilities, intelligence, and achievement

holistic mark a general-impression mark given after one reading

integrated program a term used in three different ways: (1) a program where there is a blend of all aspects of English reading, writing, listening, speaking, viewing, and valuing; (2) an individualized program related to the personal growth, skills, and cultural needs of the individual student; (3) a program coordinated with other aspects of a student's program: art, music, science, and so on.

instruction the established plan of actions and specific content specifically chosen to enable learning

learning log day-to-day written records of what is done in a particular subject area, what and how students are learning, and how they feel about what they're doing

learning through language also referred to as "language across the curriculum," this approach to the learning/teaching environment recognizes that language is intrinsic to thinking and learning; among the basic principles is the realization that students need to "think aloud" in their own informal talk or style of writing in order to fully understand concepts; during the talking and writing processes, concepts are examined, analyzed, reformulated, and defined in a personal and individual manner.

literacy the ability to read and write; extended today to include the processing of information from all sources and systems, including electronic and microelectronic

literature writing of high quality and significance because of a successful integration of components such as style, organization, language, and theme

"making meaning" the recognition that the act of processing language involves more than the communicating or recording of experience; through language we tend to construct our sense of things by clarifying, discovering, assessing, reflecting on, resolving, and refining what we really think and feel about experience.

media literacy the ability to analyze and reflect on the ways in which media events are formulated and how they function

mentor a trusted and experienced person who takes a personal and direct interest in the development and education of someone younger and less experienced

metacognition the study of thought processes

modelling the act of serving as an example of behavior: for example, a teacher reads during independent reading periods, displays a genuine courtesy toward others and a respect for individual differences, or demonstrates revision strategies using a piece of his or her own writing

peer-evaluation the process whereby an individual from the learner's peer group assesses the effectiveness of the learner's progress toward and attainment of specific goals; usually a component of formative evaluation

performance criteria standards for evaluation based on demonstration of skills or a work portfolio

personal response an instance where students begin an explication of and reflection on material with their own idiosyncratic, immediate, and spontaneous impressions, reactions, and questions where and when they arise; includes the recognition that our listening, speaking, reading, writing, viewing, and thinking processes are directed toward the making of meaning

personal writing writing about issues and events that have arisen from an individual's daily life or interests; also, any writing that involves a student to such an extent that he or she is independently motivated to complete the experience

pre-writing (rehearsing) activities and experiences occurring before the actual writing begins; includes talking, reading, picture-making, and making informal responses

project an extended school assignment, such as a research investigation, a formal experiment, or an elaborate collection

proofreading the final editing stage prior to publication

readability the degree to which the style of writing contributes to the understanding of written material

readalouds any material read aloud, usually by the teacher (Students of all ages should be read to regularly; readalouds should comprise both fiction and non-fiction and should be drawn from a variety of genres.)

reading as process the recognition that reading is an active, personal, and recursive process integral to an individual's ongoing investigation into experience and that the process requires the integration of listening, speaking, writing, viewing, and thinking for reading to be fully effective

response journal a notebook, folder, or electronic file in which students record their personal reactions to, questions about, and reflections on what they read, view, listen to, and discuss in addition to how they go about reading, viewing, listening, and discussing

response theory the proposition that understanding best begins with students explicating and reflecting on text with their own idiosyncratic, immediate, and spontaneous impressions, reactions, and questions where and when they arise

revision the act of substituting, adding, deleting, and reordering words, phrases, sections, and ideas usually with the intent of improving the text

risk taking the internalized understanding that mistakes and approximations are good; the freedom to experiment, extend the known, or try something new without unduly worrying about failing or being wrong

rubric in education, a guideline, set of rules, or detailed criteria

scribe one who transcribes the words of another

self-evaluation the process whereby the learner sets specific personal goals, determines the criteria by which progress toward and attainment of those goals is judged, and assesses the effectiveness of the learning process; the ultimate goal of all evaluation

standardized test a test with established norms to enable comparisons, for example, the Stanford-Binet Intelligence Scale

summative evaluation a process that usually employs comparative standards and judgments in order to make an overall decision (e.g., any assessment made and recorded for report card purposes)

textbook a book with specific subject matter used in schools as a learning/teaching aid

usage the customary or preferred way of using specific items of language in such areas as pronunciation, vocabulary, and syntax

webbing a commonly used method of graphically linking and organizing associated concepts, thoughts, symbols, and related activities

writing process the recursive and blended elements of writing: pre-writing, writing, post-writing: includes writing for real audiences other than the teacher and for purposes other than summative evaluation

zero tolerance a formal policy in which a code of conduct is strictly enforced; all infractions, regardless of seriousness or justification, are punished.

Selected Bibliography

Allington, Richard L., and Patricia M. Cunningham. *Schools That Work: Where All Children Read and Write.* Boston, MA: Addison Wesley, 1997.

Barnes, Douglas. *From Communication to Curriculum.* 2d ed. Portsmouth, NH: Boynton Cook/Heinemann, 1992.

Brownlie, Faye, and Judith King. *Learning in Safe Schools: Creating Classrooms Where All Students Belong.* Markham, ON: Pembroke Publishers, 2000.

Dishon, Dee, and Pat Wilson O'Leary. *Guidebook for Cooperative Learning: Techniques for Creating More Effective Schools.* 3d ed. Holmes Beach, FL: Learning Publications, 1998.

Elkind, David. *The Hurried Child: Growing Up Too Fast Too Soon.* 3d ed. Cambridge, MA: Perseus Publishing, 2001.

Flurkey, Alan D., ed. *On the Revolution of Reading: The Selected Writings of Kenneth S. Goodman.* Portsmouth, NH: Heinemann, 2003.

Fullan, Michael, and Amy Hargreaves. *What's Worth Fighting for Out There?* Toronto: Ontario Public School Teachers' Federation, 1998. (Published in the United States by Teachers College Press, 1998)

Graves, Donald H. *Discover Your Own Literacy.* Portsmouth, NH: Heinemann, 1990.

Graves, Richard L. *Writing, Teaching, Learning: A Sourcebook.* Portsmouth, NH: Heinemann, 1999.

Henchley, Norman. *Schools That Make a Difference: Final Report.* Kelowna, BC: Society for the Advancement of Excellence in Education (SAEE), 2001.

Kajder, Sara B. *The Tech-Savvy English Classroom.* Portland, ME: Stenhouse Publishers, 2003.

Oosterhof, Albert. *Classroom Applications of Educational Measurement.* Upper Saddle River, NJ: Prentice Hall/Pearson Education, 2001.

Parsons, Les. *Response Journals Revisited.* Markham, ON: Pembroke Publishers, 2001.

Rigby, Ken. *Stop the Bullying: A Handbook for Schools.* Markham, ON: Pembroke Publishers, 2001.

Smith, Frank. *Insult to Intelligence: The Bureaucratic Invasion of Our Classrooms.* New York: Arbor House, 1986.

Sweeney, Diane. *Learning Along the Way.* Portland, ME: Stenhouse Publishers, 2003.

Wiseman, Rosalind. *Queen Bees and Wannabes: Helping Your Daughter Survive Cliques, Gossip, Boyfriends, and Other Realities of Adolescence.* New York: Three Rivers Press, 2003.

Index